Unspoken

Also available in the Stolen Lives series

Taken, Michelle Pearson with Eve Hatton

Unspoken

The Silent Truth Behind My Lifelong Trauma as a Forced Adoptee

LIZ HARVIE WITH EVE HATTON

MARDLE

First published in 2023 by Mardle Books
15 Church Road
London, SW13 9HE
www.mardlebooks.com

Text © 2023 Liz Harvie

Paperback ISBN 9781837700462
eBook ISBN 9781837700479

A CIP catalogue record for this book
is available from the British Library.

Every reasonable effort has been made to trace
copyright-holders of material reproduced in this book,
but if any have been inadvertently overlooked the publishers
would be glad to hear from them.

Printed in the UK
10 9 8 7 6 5 4 3 2 1

I dedicate this book to Claire, the girl who never was, who never had the chance to be. I try to keep you alive, to keep you with me at my side. Please know that I will never leave you.

I also dedicate this book to my family:

To Grace
My first child, the daughter I secretly longed for. You have brought me intense joy from the moment I looked into your eyes. Now eighteen and about to go out into the world, you leave me as a young woman – self-assured, reliable, with a wisdom beyond your years, with integrity, passion, dedication and a brilliant mastery of the English language. Grace, you have been at my side throughout this process, casting your incredibly gifted eye over each chapter. Finally, thank you for the greatest gift you could have given to me – motherhood.

To Isabel
My second daughter, currently sixteen and growing into a wonderful young woman. You're so kind, sensitive and intuitive. The relationship we have is very special to me; we share many qualities and I see much of myself in your empathy for others. Izzy, this book is a part of your story too, and you've been so caring throughout this process, always genuinely interested in how it's going, how I'm doing. You and your sister

have seen family connections be both made and broken. But please know that my heart is so full of love for you both. You are all I ever wanted.

To Dan

To my husband, Dan – best friend turned life partner and soulmate. You are the strength to my vulnerability, the confidence to my insecurity. You love me in spite of my broken parts, you see them all and let them be. Our love is unconditional – it's a love that allows space for the more difficult emotions, that makes room for mistakes, that affords difficult conversations. It's a love full of laughter and silliness, one that holds fast through tough times. Thank you for loving me, for *choosing* me. You are my everything.

Contents

Prologue: Maybe?

Birmingham Hippodrome, October 1983
Thank goodness it's dark in here; nobody will see if I cry. No one will hear my shuddery breaths, not while the music and singing's going on.

Please, let this song end.

Below on the stage, Annie is sitting on the ledge of a pretend dormitory window, singing about her mummy and daddy who left her at this grimy orphanage. Her friends sit around her on their beds, listening.

The song is called 'Maybe', so it says in the show's programme. It's a sad, lonely song and I wish it would end, but it's echoing around me in the sooty darkness, its words pinching my heart. There's a lump in my throat, like a chewy caramel sweet that I can't swallow. My eyes sting as tears come, turning Annie into a watery blur of ragged clothes and frothy tangerine hair.

Annie is wondering what her parents are like. She imagines them to be young and clever. Good people who messed up only once when they dumped her at the orphanage as a baby. Her voice is big and brash, and it makes the scenery wobble as she pleads for her mummy and daddy to come back for her.

1

I try not to blink, try to ignore the lump stuck in my throat, but this song is painful. It's too familiar. Too 'close to home', as grown-ups say.

I don't see anybody else in the audience crying, but I understand just how Annie feels. I feel her sadness, her loneliness, her loss. She could be me; she looks around my age (I'm going to be ten in January). I was also abandoned as a baby. My real mummy couldn't keep me, so she gave me up – then I was taken away and given to a family neither of us knew.

I'm just like Annie. Only my story isn't made up. *It's real.*

My adoptive parents, the people I *call* Mummy and Daddy, brought me to see this show. My little brother Andrew is with us – he's adopted too. We're a pretend family of four, sitting in a row.

Unlike Annie, I'm lucky not to be in an orphanage, though. We live in a lovely house with a pretty garden full of roses. I don't wear rags either. Today, Mummy's put me in a wool, tartan dress with a lacy collar and cuffs. I *hate* this dress – it itches like mad against my skin.

I'm very lucky to be able to go to ballet and tennis lessons, and I always get lovely toys on my birthday. But my birthday always makes me sad inside. All the presents in the world can't replace the one thing I wish for: to see my real mummy. To feel her warm arms around me.

Will she come back for me one day, maybe realising that she made a mistake giving me away?

Annie stops singing for a moment and hops down from the window ledge. The music softens while she tucks her orphan friends into their beds, and I hear a twisty crackle of sweet wrapper – that's Mummy, unwrapping another Chocolate Eclair as the spotlight brings Annie to the front of the stage. She's singing again now, dreaming of the day her parents come

2

to collect her. She hopes they'll be there when she wakes up tomorrow. The lump is back. I blink, letting my tears plop onto my itchy dress.

Why did she give me away?

Suddenly, clattering applause brings me back. Mummy and Daddy are clapping hard and slowly, the way they always do at concerts. I clap too, try another smile, but my eyes are swimming. I feel relieved, but also sad that nobody else in my family turned to look at my face, not even to check for a reaction.

The applause dies, then Annie is back, along with her orphan pals, all slamming their metal buckets on the floor to the beat of 'It's the Hard-Knock Life'.

1

Chosen

'You're *special*, Elizabeth. Your father and I, well, we … *chose* you. We're your mummy and daddy.'

My adoptive mum melted into her velvet armchair, positioned beside the faux coal fire that burned all year round and directly opposite the television. Mum's habitual evening soap-viewing spot.

I was on the little tasselled footstool that matched her armchair, a picture developing like a Polaroid photograph in my five-year-old mind. Ghostly at first, then vivid and permanent. I visualised a yellowy hospital room packed with rows upon rows of bassinets holding babies swaddled in blankets. I imagined Mum and Dad, perusing those serried babies, umming and ah-ing until they arrived at a pink-blanketed newborn and deciding, 'Yes, I think we'll take this one.'

I looked up at Mum and she smiled into her blouse, fingering the pearls at her throat. 'Yes, that's right. You're special, Elizabeth,' she repeated. 'You're *chosen*.' Her words hung heavily in the room with the post-dinner aroma of canned creamed chicken and rice.

Special, chosen, special, chosen.

What had I asked to prompt Mum's confusing response? I can't remember my question verbatim, but it was something along the lines of, 'Who's my real mummy – and why did she give me away?' A question I'd asked many times before now.

I sat there for a moment, still trying to assimilate this 'chosen' concept. Only I couldn't get my head around it; all I could see were those rejected babies, waiting to be 'chosen'. The idea also conjured thoughts of a shopping experience. Like going to some kind of 'baby' supermarket and bringing home an infant another customer had taken back as 'unsuitable' or 'not fit for purpose'. And again, I remember thinking, as I felt the side of my face growing pink from the heat of the fire: *why would a mother give her baby away? Why did* my *mummy give me away?* There must've been something inherently wrong with me.

'But why—'

At once, our many clocks sounded, interrupting my thoughts: a deep, wise-sounding toll from the belly of the grandfather in the hallway; individual tinkling chimes from antique French timepieces.

Bing-bong, ding-dong, throughout the entire house, signalling 6.30 p.m.

Mum looked at her watch, pulled back her head, her smile shrinking to an 'ooh' expression. She nodded at the television. 'Oh, Elizabeth, be a good girl and put ITV on, would you? *Crossroads* is about to start.'

I wanted to shout, 'No!' I wanted to stay and talk about my birth mother. I wanted answers, the *truth*. But as I was fast learning, the subject of my beginnings would forever be the big elephant in the room in my adoptive home.

Deflated, I got up, padded across the lounge in my doily socks, and pushed the clunky button that boomed the fictional *Crossroads* Motel into our lounge.

'I love you, Mummy,' I said, as I headed out of the door. I was always seeking validation from my adoptive parents.

'Yes, we love you too, Elizabeth,' said Mum. And off I went to play with my Girl's World, alone, in *my* world, at the kitchen table.

Life continued, my questions left unanswered, the clocks ticking and chiming.

* * *

As far back as I can remember, I knew I was adopted. Instinct told me so – mentally *and* physically. I had this strange feeling inside: a deep, unfathomable yearning for my maternal mother – for her smell and touch and voice and love. I was forever daydreaming about what she looked like.

Mum would delight in telling the story of how she had broken the news of my adoption to me. I was just two at the time and, like all significant, poignant discussions that would happen in our family over the years, this event occurred in our lounge, during afternoon tea with 'Aunty' June, who was then heavily pregnant.

'Oh, we did laugh,' Mum would routinely say. 'I said to you, "Look Elizabeth, Aunty June has a baby in her tummy," and, just like that, you toddled over to Aunty June and lifted her dress. You were looking for her baby. You were so sweet. And that's when I told you, Elizabeth, "You came out of another lady's tummy – but *I'm* your mummy".'

I don't remember that occasion, but I can clearly picture the scene: the scrupulously polished glass of the coffee table, draped in a crisp embroidered cloth. Mum would have got her best China out, biscuits and cakes would have been arranged on little plates, the milk would have been in a China jug, the sugar in a China bowl, the display watched by bonneted Royal Doulton lady figurines who never moved from that coffee table.

So, apparently that's how I learned about my genes, my history – by looking for a baby beneath Aunty June's dress as she and Mum sipped tea and cooed at my inquisitiveness.

I suppose I'm glad Mum at least admitted I hadn't grown in her womb; many adoptees never learn this truth until much later in life. But announcing, 'You came from another lady's tummy,' knowing a two-year-old couldn't fire back awkward questions, doesn't seem entirely fair to me now. Looking back, I think Mum tricked me, burying that all-important conversation in a 'humorous' anecdote.

As a little girl I often asked myself, *why did I come out of another lady's tummy? What does this all mean?* Aunty June wasn't even related to Mum or Dad. She was a family friend, but Mum made me call most of her close female friends 'aunty', like some fabricated family. My aunts, uncles, cousins and grandparents were lovely people and they were kind to me, but I was always aware that they weren't my blood relatives.

Still, I was a curious child and I'd continue to ask the people I called Mummy and Daddy – and later, Mum and Dad – about my 'real' parents, even though I'd invariably receive their rehearsed answers: 'Your birth parents were young and unmarried. They couldn't look after you, so they gave you to parents who could *properly* look after you.' And, of course, that customary, 'You're special, you're chosen.' At times, it felt as though my adoptive parents were reciting from a script, and I remember feeling dissatisfied. I've always acknowledged how tricky those conversations must have been for Mum and Dad, but they never asked, 'How do you feel?' or 'Does it make you sad?' As a child I wanted more than simple answers to my questions; I wanted dialogue, interaction, connection. I was hurting and needed to *talk*. I didn't want to be 'chosen'.

8

In those early years, I knew little about my entrance into this world other than its date, 11 January 1974. I had no idea how much I weighed or the time of my birth – morning, afternoon, just before midnight, perhaps? Did I have my mother's features – or was I the spit of my father? Was I born with a thick mop of hair? All I had to go on was a framed baby photograph of me on the wall going up the stairs. The picture captures me at around ten months old, sporting an auburn ducktail. But was I actually *born* with auburn hair? If so, when did it turn white-blonde? I didn't even know where I was born, although I assumed it must've been near Harborne, Birmingham, where I lived with my adoptive family.

Harborne, if you've never been there, was – and still is – a charming West Midlands Victorian suburb. Imagine beautiful leafy avenues, schools rated 'outstanding' by Ofsted, a cricket club, a bowling green and a duck pond.

Mum and Dad, both born during the early years of the Second World War, had grown up a few miles away in West Bromwich, in the heart of the industrial Black Country.

Mum, a middle child between two brothers, never spoke much about her childhood, but she did relay anecdotes like playing football with her brothers, climbing trees and scrumping apples from neighbours' gardens. 'Elizabeth, you wouldn't believe it, but I was a proper tomboy,' she'd say.

Observing Mum when she recalled such stories – her hair dyed a muted apricot and always lacquered firmly into place – no, I couldn't picture Mum as a tomboy. Not for one second.

Mum's teenage years were blighted by tragedy when her father passed away, when she had just turned fourteen. I believe he died of tuberculosis, but this is all I know about my late adoptive grandfather as I think Mum found it too difficult to speak about her trauma.

I'm sure the death of my granddad also shattered his wife's heart – Mum's mum, my doting adoptive grandmother, dear, sweet Nanny Mac.

After her husband died, Nanny Mac's sister, Dot, moved in, the idea being she'd help her grieving sister to raise her three children. Apparently, Aunty Dot was a harsh, formidable force who ruled with an iron fist. Mum and her brothers subsequently endured a strict regime at the hands of their aunt.

Nanny Mac lived in a semi-detached house nestled in a horseshoe cul-de-sac. According to Mum, the house always felt chilly and damp, which probably explains why she feels the cold so much. Even at the height of summer, Mum would blast the fire in the lounge while the rest of us sweltered in T-shirts. Our house was like an oven inside.

Mum didn't need to search far before finding Dad; he lived across the road with his parents and brother in a house mirroring Nanny Mac's. I don't know much about my adoptive parents' courting days because, again, Mum and Dad never spoke much about the past. This much I do know, though: they met as young adults, then married at a West Bromwich church in June 1969. Mum wore a simple ivory dress and a veil comprising a headdress embellished with a satin rose. Every now and then, Mum would get that veil, which she'd kept as a keepsake, out of the wardrobe for me. I thought it smelled of time and dust, like the olden days.

Another souvenir from my adoptive parents' big day was their photo album. I would spend hours thumbing through those black-and-white pictures, studying the fashions, settings and guests and noting the likenesses between relations of Mum and Dad. I love old photographs; the history and stories behind them fascinate me. Sometimes, though, I'd look at those pictures and realise, *I can't see myself* – these *are not my people*. And once more, I'd drift into a reverie about my birth parents.

Sadly, Mum and Dad were unable to conceive their own children, so they adopted me via the Church of England Children's Society – now known as the Children's Society – in early 1974. Two-and-a-half years later, Mum and Dad adopted my little brother, Andrew. He was six weeks old. Tabitha, our tabby cat, completed our family.

In the eyes of the Church of England Children's Society, and society in general, we were the 'perfect' middle-class unit. Dad was a high-flying finance director and Mum, a housewife, who also volunteered as a magistrate once a week. They owned a four-bedroom property in the suburbs of Birmingham and went to church every Sunday. On paper, Mum and Dad ticked all the right boxes as adoptive parents.

Andrew and I were fortunate to live in a lovely home – a 1930s' period house fronted by a horseshoe drive, an arched porch and a polished brass doorknob on the front door which you could see your face in. At the back, the house opened out onto a perfectly manicured garden, alive in spring and summer with nodding roses, hydrangeas the colour of Parma Violets and rhododendrons in ruby, cerise and powdery pinks. Bracketing the lawn were two elliptical flower beds, one blooming with Elizabeth rosettes, the other with Andrew roses. Mum told us she and Dad bought and planted those roses as they matched our names.

Inside, the house was like a moment in time, almost every item of furniture being a vintage piece bought from an antiques fair, while framed watercolours depicting quaint country landscapes decorated the walls. And whichever room you went into, you had to pass through the square hallway, complete with its original 1930s' wood panelling and home to our proud grandfather clock, which my father carefully tended every few months. A carpet the colour of red wine that drove Mum mad because it 'showed up all the bits' covered the stairs.

My favourite room in the house was my bedroom, which sat above the kitchen at the back of the house, overlooking the garden. This space was my sanctuary; I used to love gazing out of the bay window, inhaling the perfume of the climbing roses below in summer, or sitting next to the radiator during winter, watching the garden turn Narnia-esque in silent snowfalls. I remember looking up through that window at a sky full of white, searching for the biggest, dancing snowflake. I would be there for ages, lost in the silent magic of the snow.

Andrew and I never wanted for anything. We had plenty of toys: Play-Doh, Mr Frosty, Painting by Numbers and my cherished doll's house. I played with Sindy and Barbie dolls and Andrew had his Lego and Transformers toys. We went to piano and swimming lessons, and I took ballet and acting classes. Mum and Dad took us on lovely holidays to five-star resorts in the South of France, Bermuda, Tenerife and Gran Canaria. I have fond memories from those holidays, and I appreciated everything my adoptive parents provided. I still do. But, for me, there was something missing. What I craved was warmth, an understanding. I realise now I was trying to make connections with my adoptive parents that simply weren't there. I wanted to talk about my adoption and how I felt. Looking back, maybe Mum and Dad carried a lot of grief regarding their infertility, which is understandable.

Andrew and I were close; I felt protective of him. He was like me – an outsider, an alien – so we stuck together, but we never spoke about being adopted. We just didn't, because again, adoption seemed to be a taboo subject in our house. I went through the motions of family life, but inside, I was often screaming, 'Hello, I'm here, can you see me?'

Mum followed a rigid regime at home, her focus seemingly being on the veneer of our family: how we behaved and looked to the outside world. Whenever we were expecting guests, Mum would get Andrew and me to help clean and tidy the already immaculate house. This ritual involved us crawling up and down the stairs, picking all the 'bits' off the maroon carpet by hand. It was also my job to dust the spindles of the eight dark-wood dining-room chairs and to polish the mirrored glass coffee table in the lounge. Although I think I spent more time pulling funny faces and giggling at my reflection in the glass than I did cleaning it. Anything to liven up that task.

It wouldn't matter who our visitors were – relatives, neighbours or old family friends like 'Aunty' June – everything in the house had to be just so. I'll never forget one Boxing Day evening when I plonked a bottle of mayonnaise on the dinner table in front of our aunts, uncles and cousins. Mum eyed the condiment as though it were a tarantula picking its way across the table, her eyebrows rocketing to her hairline. 'Elizabeth, whatever are you thinking?' she said, shooing me with sharp, rapid flicks of her fingers. 'Go and put that in a little pot, a little ramekin.' I did what I was told, thinking, *this is totally bonkers.*

Mum always ensured Andrew and I were immaculately turned out, particularly so on Sundays when we attended the morning service at the local United Reformed Church in West Bromwich. Mum would lay out our clothes, usually a frou-frou dress and frilly socks for me and a little suit and tie for Andrew. Then off we'd go to church, trussed up like chickens.

I can't remember my first day at school, which is a shame as this event is monumental for many children. But to be fair, I was practically still a toddler when I started at Edgbaston Church of England College for Girls in September 1977. My nursery teacher, along with Mum and Dad, decided I was intelligent enough to start school aged three rather than wait another year, so I was placed in a class with girls who were soon to be five.

I remained at Edgbaston Church of England College for Girls until I turned sixteen.

One thing I'll never forget about the girls' private 'college', now a mixed-sex school called St George's, was the uniform: a dark-brown and seventies' orange ensemble involving a mushroom hat, pleated skirt, cream blouse, stripy tie and blazer bearing the school's crest.

Dress code aside, I mostly enjoyed my early school years. I loved the school dinners, especially the gooey puddings like chocolate concrete, encrusted with hundreds and thousands, or cornflake tart, spread thick with synthetic strawberry jam and swimming in lashings of pink custard, and the smell of chips that filled the dining hall on Fridays was to die for. Some of my peers thought my appetite for the school food was a bit strange, but to me it was comfort.

My fondest school memories include playing outside with friends during the lunch hour in summer. As soon as the bell rang, we would charge out to the playing field, where we'd sit cross-legged in the sunshine and make daisy chains. On other days, we'd venture right to the bottom of the big field to pet the friendly horses over the fence or play in the shadow of an ancient oak tree reminiscent of the Tree Tots Family Tree House toy all kids wished for in the late 1970s, the one with the little drop-down swing and rooms between branches where the Tree Tot toy figures lived and played. My friends and I loved that Family Tree House, always the top item listed in our letters to Father Christmas. Meanwhile, how lucky we were to have a real, life-size version of the toy on our doorstep. We loved playing there; we would pretend the tree was our house. We made broomsticks from branches and twigs to sweep floors of imaginary rooms circling the gnarly tree trunk. Those truly were idyllic times. Being with nature, immersed in my imagination, was a welcome distraction for me.

As far as I knew at the time, I was the only adoptee at my school, and this was something I was always conscious of. Whenever I went to friends' houses for parties or sleepovers, I'd find myself analysing the dynamics between them and their parents, especially their mothers.

Our closest family friends lived next door to us: Vanessa, her husband Bob and their two daughters, Anna and Jess, who were a year older and younger than me respectively. I found it as enjoyable as I found it difficult playing with Anna and Jess in their house. They were allowed to make 'potions' in the bathroom sink, mixing shaving foam with bubble bath, shower gel, talcum powder, toothpaste and any other toiletries they could find. I would have loved to have done this at home, but Mum would never have allowed it. The mess alone would have been unacceptable.

I'd notice particularly how my friends bonded with their mothers. To me, their connections appeared relaxed and authentic … biological. And while I couldn't fully acknowledge this at the time, it hurt me to watch those real, loving mother-daughter relationships.

The atmosphere in our home was more stilted. I can't remember Mum and Dad being particularly affectionate towards each other. They wouldn't snuggle together on the sofa, both preferring to sit separately in their respective armchairs.

Mum was a stickler for routine, especially during the week. Dinner happened at 6 p.m. on the dot and would invariably be Mum's signature creation of 'rice 'n' things', a combination of creamed canned meat and rice strewn with shrivelled peas and tiny cubes of red pepper. Once we'd eaten, the dishwasher had been loaded, and all evidence of the evening meal had been put away, Mum would head to the lounge to watch her soaps while Dad took himself off to his study to tinker with his antique clocks and listen to classical music.

My adoptive parents did enjoy a thriving social life, though. They had a solid circle of friends composed of a few other couples, a happy group they called The Gang. They did everything together, The Gang, from coffee mornings and concerts to theatre trips, golfing weekends and city breaks.

Dad's job also required him to attend a number of dinner-dance dos with Mum. I have strong memories of sitting on their bed, watching them prepare for the evening ahead, captivated by the process. There'd be Mum at the dressing table, putting her heated rollers in, bending her arms this way and that. I liked to sort the roller clips into colours. I knew which one went with which size roller and I would pass them silently to my mother as she did her hair. Rollers done, she'd apply her make-up. I would watch intently. Always in the same order, the same sounds accompanied the routine. The clickety-clack, tip-tap, snap percussion of compacts being opened and closed. Eyelids aflicker against light strokes of a mascara wand. Make-up done, Mum would then meticulously unravel her rollers before assembling her curls into a cloud-shaped helmet, ready to be blasted with hairspray. Dad would come into the room, sharp in his dinner suit, immaculately shaven and smelling all soapy. He'd fasten his cufflinks and tie while Mum misted her wrists, neck and décolletage with Nina Ricci's L'Air du Temps, a heady aroma of carnations and spices. I'd be fascinated to know what outfit Mum had chosen – usually a conservative, shoulder-padded evening dress – and equally intrigued to know where she and Dad were going. Their preparations complete, I'd watch Mum and Dad walk down the stairs, engulfed in an extra-strong, almost visible fug of L'Air du Temps. And then they'd head out of the door into their mysterious grown-up nocturnal world, leaving Andrew and me with our babysitter, the wonderful Nanny Mac.

I adored Nanny Mac. I associate many of my memories, particularly good ones, with smells, and Nanny Mac's scent was especially reminiscent of comfort. A gentle and homely blend of dolly mixture sweets and talcum powder. Nanny Mac had the most beautiful, brilliant snow-white hair, soft as candy floss, and a smile that came straight from her heart was as evident in her eyes. She never went anywhere without her patent fifties-style handbag, with its sturdy brass clasp that shut with a satisfying click.

We visited Nanny Mac in West Bromwich every Sunday after church. I loved going to her house. She was such a wonderful soul, happy and funny and always playing with Andrew and me – or asking us questions about school and our activities. Whenever we arrived at Nanny Mac's house, she'd wrap me in a cosy hug, kiss my cheek, and in a voice sweet as her perfume, say, 'How's my Little piccaninny?'* That was Nanny Mac's nickname for me – after the 1915 Gladys Rice song she used to sing to me, 'Go to Sleep My Little Pickaninny'. Bless Nanny Mac, I don't think she knew all the words to that lullaby, but she'd la, la, la her way through those missing lines. I'd rest my head on her soft shoulder, close my eyes, inhale her sugary fragrance and drift away to a place of comfort and calm.

After greeting us with kisses and cuddles, Nanny Mac would motion for us to follow her. 'There's a little something in the cupboard for you both,' she'd say, and Andrew and I would pitter-patter excitedly across the dining room to her dark-wood sideboard, pull open its carved doors and marvel, as Nanny Mac's aroma engulfed us again in concentrated form: dolly mixtures, humbugs, lime-green boiled sweets with chocolate

---

* Now considered offensive when used by a white person of a black child.

centres, all encased in white paper bags and bought from a sweet shop whose measures still came in ounces and pounds. It's funny; even though we knew what we'd find in Nanny Mac's cupboard, those pretty sweets never failed to delight us. We'd be ecstatic, hurriedly popping as many as possible into our mouths before Mum could object.

It was little things like dolly mixtures and playing upstairs at Nanny Mac's that thrilled me as a child – more so than toys. In Nanny Mac's second bedroom I'd rummage through her jewellery box, a magpie's dream haul packed with twinkly trinkets like crystal necklaces that threw glittery disco-ball patterns over the walls and ceiling when the light hit the beads. Some of her jewellery was decades old at least and I imagined the stories each piece held. *Who bought this brooch for Nanny? Did she buy this ring for herself? Or did she buy it second-hand? If so, who owned it before? Or maybe it was left to her by her mummy? I wonder what Nanny's mummy was like?* And on I'd go, touching and smelling each charm, stories flickering like Super-8 films in my head. This was my escapism.

Often on those Sundays we'd take a run out in the car and go for walks in the Lickey or Clent Hills. I particularly loved seeing the millions of bluebells that carpet the Clent Hills in springtime. But for me, the best moments of those jaunts happened when we drove home. In the back seat, I'd cuddle up to Nanny Mac and feel a rush of excitement hearing the comfy thud-click of her handbag opening, releasing its scent – still sugary sweet but infused with leather. 'Shall we make a dolly?' Nanny Mac would ask, retrieving a freshly washed cotton handkerchief and a piece of ribbon from the depths of her handbag.

I'd nod rapidly into her shoulder. 'Yes please, Nanny Mac,' and watch, mesmerised, as she folded and tied and knotted until magically, the handkerchief became a doll in a long floral dress. 'There you go, my little piccaninny,' Nanny Mac would say as the dolly appeared to float down into my hands, and then she'd start singing the Gladys Rice lullaby, all the way back to West Bromwich.

My relationship with Nanny Mac meant the world to me. My other Nanny was quite different. She was often nagging or shouting at poor old Granddad and didn't smile very much. I felt there was little warmth for me there. Thinking about it now, I wonder whether she suffered from depression, but I often found visits to Dad's parents difficult – the fraught atmosphere was upsetting. One scene I recall at my grandparents' house unnerved me.

It was a typical Sunday visit, and I was sitting in the living room with Mum, Dad, Andrew, Nanny and my Uncle Geoff, Dad's younger brother, who also lived there while Granddad cooked lunch in the kitchen. An incessant roar of chanting, clapping, whistles and klaxon honks poured from the telly. The football was always on whenever we visited Dad's parents. Either that, or *Bullseye*. A few minutes later the kitchen door slid open and in came Granddad, a big smile on his face. 'Lunch is almost ready,' he said, 'I hope you're all h—'

Nan snapped round in her chair, eyes ablaze, framed by her heavy tortoiseshell glasses. 'Shut that bloomin' door! You're letting the draught in.'

Those harsh words seemed to pass through Granddad, who pointed his forehead at the television. 'What's the score?' he said. Then he turned and headed back to the kitchen, sliding the door closed again. Nan carried on watching the match as though nothing had happened, while I felt heavy inside, deeply upset at what I'd just witnessed. How could a woman speak to her husband like that? And I started to wonder, amid the cacophonic football chorus, *did my birth family behave like this?*

Suffice to say, I didn't bond with Dad's mum as I did with Nanny Mac. The relationship I shared with her felt so natural, maternal. Sadly, I would never share the same closeness with Mum. She didn't even *smell* like a mum to me, something I've recently discovered is a phenomenon among fellow adoptees I've met – our adoptive mothers just didn't smell right to us.

Growing up, I was a daddy's girl. I definitely got along better with Dad than I did with Mum. When I was old enough to understand chess, Dad would play it with me, but Mum never did. Whenever I asked her to, she'd sigh and say, 'Oh, go and ask your father, Elizabeth.'

Dad enjoyed his hobbies – collecting antique clocks, listening to classical music and golfing. He was also a good amateur photographer; he took some lovely shots of Andrew and me, often in our garden or during our holidays abroad. Although, revisiting these pictures as I write this, I notice how sad I look in many of them. In one snap, taken when I was around four, I'm wearing a rainbow-checked sundress, its straps tied in neat bows on my suntanned shoulders. My hair is in a tidy topknot, with wispy tendrils curling past my ears. If a stranger were to look at this picture they'd probably say, 'Oh, what a sweet little girl.' They wouldn't question my anxious, wistful expression as I gaze not at the camera but into the distance.

Another picture shows me aged about eleven, sitting on our garden bench in a baby-pink Sunday School-style dress that looks too young for me. My pose is stilted and stiff – straight back, hands resting inside each other in my lap, my frilly-socked ankles crossed. Again, I'm wearing the same faraway gaze. I just look lost.

Only looking at these pictures now do I remember how lost I really was growing up, despite living in a safe and comfortable environment.

From an early age, my imagination was my diversion and, fortunately, I was good at entertaining myself. I loved, as I still do, bonding with nature.

One summer afternoon, when I was five or six, I leant out of my bedroom window to find the climbing roses peppered with ladybirds. This wasn't an unusual sight – roses do attract insects – but I suddenly felt compelled to nurture these little bugs. *You magical flying creatures must live with me*, I decided, so, one by one, I gently cupped the ladybirds in my hands, brought them inside and placed them in my doll's house. *Now you're safe, my little friends.* I had at least ten ladybirds living in my doll's house, crawling and fluttering amidst the miniature furniture. Occasionally, I'd hold one in my hands and watch its spotted flaps unfold and its hindwings spring out in preparation for take-off. Those gossamer wings would then beat like crazy until, ping, the ladybird launched itself from my palms and flew out of the window. I'd then follow the creature's flight path until it vanished in the sky before scooping another ladybird off the roses to check in to my doll's house.

All was going well at Chez Ladybird – until a few weeks later when I overheard Mum telling Dad, 'We appear to have an infestation of ladybirds – and they seem to be coming from Elizabeth's bedroom.' A mass clean-up operation ensued to eradicate the ladybirds. I missed them once they'd gone; they were my little pets, my friends. All I'd wanted was to nurture them.

Mum hated dirt and creepy-crawlies, especially spiders – she'd shriek the house down whenever she saw one. For this reason, she wouldn't go anywhere near our little wooden greenhouse where our gardener, Mr Bradley, grew all manner of lush fruits and vegetables.

Dear old Mr Bradley; I can still see him now. He looked like a friendly version of the grumpy Mr McGregor from Beatrix Potter's *The Tale of Peter Rabbit* in his navy overalls and muddy working boots. He always wore a cap and walked with a slight limp. Mr Bradley came twice a week and I'd beg Mum, 'Please can I take Mr Bradley his coffee?' Then I'd trot off down the garden with his black coffee and plate of biscuits and sit with him for a while in the tomato-scented greenhouse and ask him what he was growing while he cleaned his tools. I loved picking the juicy tomatoes and breathing in the ripe, green smell that lingered on my fingers.

Towards the end of the summer, Mr Bradley would deadhead the rose bushes. Excitedly, I'd ask, 'Ooh, please can I have the petals?' I'd follow him as he lolloped around the garden, picking up the clipped petals which I'd later mash up with water in a jar to make rose perfume – a hack I'd read about in my weekly *Twinkle* magazine, the 'picture paper specially for little girls' back in the day. The *Twinkle* article advised leaving the stewing petals outside at night, beneath the moon and stars, for the fragrance to develop. I remember being fascinated by that mystical element, just as I was obsessed by fairy tales and folklore. I'd lose myself in the *Flower Fairies* books by the late illustrator Cicely Mary Barker, poring over the beautiful words and pictures and imagining similar fairies might live in our garden.

Being a creative child, I was always doodling. I'd draw the same scene repeatedly, depicting a pretty cottage with duck-pond, neat vegetable garden and a winding path leading to a front door framed by roses. Even later, in my university years, I'd sketch this same scene – and I now realise what inspired this imagery. Recently, while speaking with fellow adoptees, I discovered the word 'hiraeth', defined as 'a deep longing for a person or thing which is absent or lost; yearning, nostalgia'. It confirmed the meaning behind my cottage drawing: I was expressing emotions I couldn't verbalise, a yearning for my birth parents, specifically an intense longing for my birth mother. To be 'home', whatever that meant.

Mum and Dad – Mum especially – were extremely over-protective of Andrew and me. This became suffocating as I approached my teenage years. Whenever I look at a particular photograph of my brother and me on our bikes in our driveway – I'm around eleven or twelve in the shot and wearing a black-and-white jumper knitted by Nanny Mac – I'm reminded of how restrictive Mum was at that time. 'Remember,' she'd say when Andrew and I headed out on our bikes, 'five doors down only – and stick to the pavement. No going in the road.' It became so monotonous, riding along the pavement five doors down, wheeling round, back to our house, in and out of the horseshoe drive, then performing the same circuit over and over again.

Without a doubt, life at home could be overbearing at times. There would be moments when I'd argue with Mum. After being sent to my room, as I curled in a foetal position on my bed, drenching the pillow with tears, I'd think to myself, *you're not my real mother – would she have responded in the same way?* I'd never have said that to Mum, though; I feared her reaction. Would she and Dad send me away somewhere? I'd already been abandoned once; the thought of this happening again terrified me to the core. Mum and Dad might not have been my *real* parents, and despite my often feeling like a stranger in our family, Mum and Dad were the ones who looked after me. They were, after all, my security, all I knew.

One day, I thought maybe Mum *had* abandoned me. This happened about a year after the ladybirds saga, on a shopping trip with Mum to Rackhams, the department store in

Birmingham city centre. I adored going to Rackhams, mainly for its ground-floor perfumery and make-up department. I'd gaze in awe at the glamorous ladies behind the counters, spritzing and smiling, perfectly made up. For me, walking through that section was like being in a scented paradise. It was in the haberdashery department, however, where my nightmare unfolded.

While Mum perused the zips and fastenings aisle, I wandered into another section, seduced by its rows of cards holding buttons resembling sweets. I have a vague recollection of looking at buttons that reminded me of the dolly mixtures Nanny Mac bought for us – little cubes in pastel colours when, I suddenly realised I was alone in that aisle. A rush of panic overwhelmed me, my mind awhirl with dark thoughts. *Where has my mummy gone? Where is she? Mummy's left me.* Lift music crescendoed to a warped pitch, assailing my little ears. The buttons transmogrified into menacing eyes, staring and laughing as my chest heaved with the sheer terror at being lost. *Mummy's left me.*

Tears flooding my face, I ran into the next aisle, rolls of brightly coloured fabrics blurring into a taunting rainbow ahead. As I turned the corner I saw another customer, a lady in a royal-blue coat who was studying reels of satin ribbons. What happened next is hazy in my mind, but I do remember calling out to that lady in a panicky voice, 'Help, I've lost my mummy.' I think an announcement was made over the store's Tannoy system, which ultimately reunited me with Mum, who'd been frantically pacing the aisles looking for me. I'd only been lost for a few minutes at most, but it felt like an eternity at the time.

* * *

As a child, whenever people asked me that ubiquitous question, 'What do you want to be when you grow up?' I couldn't answer. I knew I probably wanted to do something creative, but I was too young to know my options then. What I also knew, from quite early on, was that more than anything in this world I wanted to become a mum. I longed for my own baby to love and to nurture.

Soon after my seventh birthday, I asked Mum, 'How are babies made?' Her response was along the lines of, 'Oh, mummies and daddies have a special cuddle,' then I think she changed the subject. This confused me. *Surely there's more to making babies than a 'special cuddle'?* That's when I found a book, buried beneath some appliance manuals in a drawer in the kitchen – left in a subtle place for Andrew and me to discover. The title – Margaret Sheffield's *Where Do Babies Come From?* – had an illustration of a sad looking naked baby and sunflowers on its cover. Flashbacks of the pictures contained in that book make me laugh now – all I remember is the seventies-style images, the women sporting voluminous hairy triangles between their thighs. All the men had beards, too. But I was absolutely fascinated by that book, sneakily leafing through its informative pages whenever the opportunity arose, which was usually after dinner. As an adoptee, I was desperate to know about where babies came from and how they were born. One illustration in the book left a lasting impression on me. It demonstrated how we end up with a belly-button after the umbilical cord is cut. This was a huge revelation to me; suddenly, I became obsessed with my belly button. It sounds bonkers, I know, but I have memories of lying in bed and staring down at my midriff for ages, of stroking the little knot marking the spot that once connected me to my birth mother. In my mind's eye, my belly-button was the most special part on my body, one I wanted to cherish, and whenever I looked at it, I'd think, *My belly-button is the only thing I have belonging to my real mummy.*

Although initially traumatised as a baby, the impact of that preverbal trauma, for me – and for other adoptees – is lifelong. I'm hypervigilant: my fight-or-flight response is through the roof; I only have to hear a balloon pop and I shriek out loud. Such reactions are manifestations of my absolute panic at being taken from my maternal mother as a newborn. Although my mind doesn't remember this, my body does. Somebody had taken my birth mother, and I didn't know where she had gone. Every cell, fibre, bone and nerve in me remembers, and all manner of noises, smells, sensations and events can trigger this trauma within me. I was barely eight when I first experienced such a reaction.

We were at Uncle Gordon and Aunty Viv's house (Mum's younger brother and his wife) one Sunday afternoon. I always looked forward to seeing Aunty Viv. She was stunning: very Biba-esque with her bold, winged eyeliner and fluttery eyelashes. And she had this amazing long, thick, shiny chestnut hair which she'd let me brush.

As soon as we stepped into Aunty Viv and Uncle Gordon's house, Andrew went off to play with their son Adam. The boys always left me out of their games, claiming cops and robbers and trucks were 'not for girls'.

Aunty Viv smiled down at me. 'Come on, Elizabeth,' she said as the boys charged up the stairs, deliberating who would play the 'baddie', 'I'll introduce you to Ruth. You can play with her.'

I gave a polite nod, nerves and excitement brewing in my stomach. Mum had told me about Ruth, the baby who Aunty Viv was 'fostering'. 'Ruth's mummy and daddy couldn't look after her so Aunty Viv is taking care of her for a while,' she'd explained. I followed Aunty Viv upstairs, thinking, *I love babies, but what does 'fostering' mean exactly? Will Ruth be adopted like me? Will she too be 'chosen'?*

Ruth, no more than a few months old, was on her back, a tiny bundle on the cherry-blossom quilt. She had on a dress in the same pink as the bedspread, her chubby little legs kicking, frog-like, from the hem. High-pitched cooing noises came in a flurry from Aunty Viv's mouth as she lifted Ruth off the bed and turned to face me, bouncing the baby in her arms. 'Look, Ruth, this is Elizabeth. She's a big girl who's come to play with you.'

I tilted my head to one side and gave a little wave. 'Hello Ruth,' I said, while Aunty Viv put Ruth back down on the bed. 'I'll be downstairs if you need me,' said my aunt as she breezed out of the room.

Ruth seemed quite content, gurgling away. I sat on the edge of the bed and said hello to her again, trying to speak in a gentle, motherly voice. I reached for her dimpled hand, but she scrunched it up into an angry fist. Her eyes creased too, and a painful silence fell in the pink bedroom before Ruth started crying.

My heart shook with Ruth's cries. The noise frightened me. *Who is this baby? Where are her parents?* Ruth's wails intensified. Louder, faster, drowning the vroom, vroom, vroom sounds coming from Adam's room. I was paralysed by panic; I didn't know what to do. I clapped my hands over my ears. I felt sorry for Ruth. I wanted to help her, but I couldn't stand the noise of her distress. Equally, I didn't want to leave her alone. My throat tightened with sadness. *Ruth wants her real mummy. Where is her mummy? Where's my real mummy?*

Just then, Aunty Viv came back into the room. 'There, there,' she said and, in one swift movement, scooped Ruth off the bed, shush-shushing and rocking her screams away. I sat there, staring at Ruth's flushed wet face, aware that her cries were fading but still hearing her haunting screams. I too was crying inside, but I couldn't take my eyes off Ruth as I realised that she and I were the same: two unwanted children, crying for our mothers. Not that the grown-ups in the house at that point would have acknowledged that. There would be no connection made between me and Ruth, no thought for the similarities in our beginnings; our bond to them was invisible. Nobody said, or even thought, a word. It simply didn't occur to them. I felt that my reaction to that scene was totally different from that of the grown-ups: to them, Ruth was simply a crying baby. So I swallowed my feelings that afternoon. It was clear to me that there should not even have been a problem, and for me to express my thoughts would have seemed inappropriate to them, ridiculous even. So, I never let them out.

Forever unspoken.

2

Is My Mum a Film Star?

This memory has never left me: I'm ten years old, pattering along the landing in our house, the claret carpet cushiony underfoot. I can hear the clocks tick-tocking as I pass Mum and Dad's bedroom on my left before skipping across to the family bathroom.

I push the door and enter the pristine space, furnished with a 1930s' sky-blue porcelain suite. It's like a hall of mirrors in here: there's a full-length mirror on the back of the door, another one looms over the bevelled pedestal basin and there is a huge, arched reflector on the wall above the bath.

The air makes my face smart, the sharp scent of Vim bathroom-cleaning powder overpowers the comfier smells of Imperial Leather soap, Vosene shampoo and Badedas Indulgent Bubble Bath Gel – my parents' staple toiletries.

This is where I come to try to look into my past.

I stand before the long mirror on the back of the door, my face a few inches away from the glass. A girl in a checked, Peter Pan-collared dress stares back at me, blonde hair fastened in a neat, low ponytail.

I raise my chin and angle my face right, left, right again, analysing my features. My chin is square-ish with a horizontal dimple below my bottom lip. *Is this what my biological father's chin looks like? Or did I get this chin from my birth mother? What about my eyes?* I stare into them – sometimes they look blue, sometimes green-ish, but they always seem to match the bathroom suite. *Does my birth mother have similar eyes? Do I look like her? Does she have the same shape face as me? Maybe I look just like her? I want to see her face. I* need *to see her face, here, in this mirror. Please, let me see you.*

I'm trying to conjure an older version of myself, hoping for some sort of magic to happen. But I can't see what I want to see. Even when I frown, smile or squint so my reflection becomes a ghostly, peachy blob, the woman who made me doesn't appear in this mirror. And when I open my eyes as wide as they'll go, all I'm left with is me. I feel so incredibly lost.

As a child, I spent countless hours in that bathroom, willing the mirror to give something back to me, constantly thinking, *where do I come from?* I wanted so badly to see my birth mother's face, the thing that that mattered so much to me – more than anything in the world.

Often, I'd catch myself staring at strangers in the street, or in a shop, asking myself, *is that her? Is that my birth mother?*

Once, Mum took me to a nearby town during the school holidays. I can't recall the name of the town, but it was a place I'd never been to before. As we walked hand in hand through the unfamiliar centre, people streaming past us like in a television drama shot, my gaze darted from one female face to the next, searching for an older version of me. I looked for fair-skinned women with blonde hair and blue eyes – these attributes were the only clues to my genes. *Maybe I was born in this town*, I thought. *Maybe my real mother is here, in this crowd, looking for me too.* Of course, I didn't voice those thoughts to Mum.

That day out with her came a couple of weeks after our family theatre trip to see *Annie*. I still couldn't understand why my adoptive parents had taken Andrew and me to see a musical about orphans. The song 'Maybe' played hauntingly in my head as I lay in bed at night, unable to sleep. Mum and Dad hadn't even noticed my swollen eyes and tear-streaked face during the interval. 'Isn't it a good show,' Mum had gushed as we'd headed to the foyer to buy ice-creams. 'Are you enjoying it?' I couldn't answer. I'd told her I needed the toilet; I wanted to be alone for a while. I sat inside the cubicle, silently asking myself the same questions as Annie: *do my real parents live nearby – or far away? Do they regret giving me away? What if my real parents turn up on our doorstep, saying they've come back for me? Would I go with them?*

On the drive home from the theatre, nobody mentioned that we'd just watched a performance about abandoned, unloved children. Mum and Dad didn't sit Andrew and me down that evening or the next day – or any other day – and say, 'How did *Annie* affect you? Did the show upset you?' It surely would've been the perfect opportunity for such a conversation. But no. Once again, it was all swept under the carpet.

Growing up, I continually questioned my identity. I was so confused. People who didn't know our family background often commented that Andrew and I looked 'nothing like one another', which was true. Andrew had light brown hair and navy eyes, and his chin was more rounded and narrower than mine. His grin was wide, like an upside-down rainbow stretching towards his temples, compared to my straight smile. But then again, why would we look alike? We were adopted.

Beyond appearances, however, Andrew and I were close. He was my little buddy at home, and we shared some characteristics and interests. We had a similar, silly sense of humour, and Andrew and I were both musical. We both played the piano, although my adoptive brother was more gifted than me. I could play classical pieces well if I followed sheet music or sometimes I'd make up compositions around a few minor chords, but Andrew was like a mini-Mozart, performing nursery rhymes by ear aged three. He also had a beautiful voice and, a few years later, he became a choirboy, singing with the Birmingham Cathedral Choristers. We both took up a second instrument: I played the oboe and Andrew, the organ. Music surrounded us.

Music became such an important part of my life. It was my comfort, my escapism – and it still is today. Playing the piano as a child, I'd wonder whether my birth parents were musically talented. My adoptive parents didn't play instruments; Mum was tone deaf, but Dad's love for classical music inspired me. Dad's job was hectic and stressful, so he cherished his moments in the evenings, after Mum had gone to bed (she always turned in before Dad), when he'd pour a glass of Glenfiddich and settle in his armchair by the stereo to play his records. The house became an oasis of calm at this time, around 9 p.m.

Before then, the dreary *Coronation Street* theme tune or the crashing doof-doofs of *EastEnders* would boom through the living room walls as Mum watched her soaps, so it was a welcome relief to hear a Beethoven symphony or a Chopin nocturne coming from that same room.

I loved these times; I'd often join Dad in the living room, transformed into a peaceful space, with the usually booming television now behind its closed, polished wooden cabinet. I'd sit beside him on my footstool and watch enthralled as he began his nightly ritual. He'd pour his whisky into a crystal tumbler, drop in a couple of ice cubes and put on a record before sitting back in his armchair, his cheeks squishing the rims of his glasses as he smiled. I'd hear the delicate sounds of ice chinking when he took his first sip of whisky – then music would float from the stereo, usually the solo trumpet notes of Mahler's *Symphony No. 5*, Dad's favourite piece, soft initially, then lifting, as other brass instruments join in, to a peak punctuated with a sharp smash of cymbals.

Dad's whisky, with its peaty smell and deep amber glow, fascinated me. One evening, as we listened to a Bach cello suite, beautiful and yearning, I pointed at Dad's glass and asked him, 'What does that taste like?'

'Here, try a little bit,' he said, proffering his tumbler.

I lifted the glass to my lips, again revelling in the sound of chiming ice, gulped a generous mouthful and gasped as the liquid travelled down my gullet. 'Gosh, how can you drink that?' I said, my throat burning. 'It's like fire.' Dad laughed, a little rumbly chuckle. I laughed too, enjoying our secret, relaxed time together – Mum would've gone mad if she knew I'd tried whisky, especially as I was only twelve. Those evenings with Dad were special to me.

Music connected us, in the same way it connected me to Andrew, enabling me to establish some semblance of a father-daughter bond. Dad would often stand outside my bedroom and listen when I practised my oboe, occasionally popping his head round the door to offer words of encouragement and praise. We had this game we'd play together that we called 'Guess the Composer'. This came later – when I was studying for my music GCSE. During our evening music sessions in the lounge, I'd turn my back to the stereo so I couldn't see which record Dad was putting on. 'Right then, Elizabeth,' he'd say proudly as the stylus touched the vinyl with a gentle crackle, 'which period of music is this from?

A few bars into the piece, I'd announce my answer: Romantic, Renaissance, Baroque … Then Dad would say, 'Yep, that's right, Elizabeth … but can you guess the composer?' And so, we'd go on, piece after piece. I always felt so proud of myself when I answered correctly.

While my early school memories are mostly good, like my special times with Dad, I struggled as I grew older. From the age of nine onwards, some of my classmates would ask me questions, such as, 'What's it like to be adopted?' or 'Why were you adopted?' Naturally, they were curious, but I found those questions difficult. I'd just shrug and tell a fib along the lines of, 'It's just like being in a normal family.' I didn't want to say, 'For some reason my real mother didn't want me, so she gave me away.' I'd been conditioned not to speak about my adoption.

One incident I remember at school was when our teacher asked us to draw our family trees. I can still see myself, sitting at my desk – watching the other girls sketching trees blossoming with 'real' relatives: parents, grandparents, aunts, cousins and so forth – staring at a blank page, thinking, *What's the point? These people are not my kin.* I did finally draw my tree, connecting Mum and Dad's families, but that lesson was challenging for me. I felt angry, as if I was living a lie, while my family carried on pretending. At the end of the class, I handed my fake lineage to my teacher, but she said nothing. I don't think she gave it a second thought that I might have found that task difficult.

A month or so later, I was sitting on the school playing field with a group of girls at lunchtime when one of them, Cara, narrowed her eyes at me, a small smirk flitting across her freckled face, and blurted, 'You don't have real parents. Your *real* mum didn't want you, so she gave you away. Your mum isn't your *real* mum.' I swallowed down my tears, my throat tightening. I heard the other girls mumbling. One echoed Cara: 'You don't have a real mum,' but I stared down into the pleats of my brown skirt, wishing the earth would swallow me whole. Then anger rose in my chest. A spiteful, burning anger I'd never experienced until now. Cara had hurt and humiliated me, and something in my ten-year-old mind told me to do the same to her. I remembered, then, that her nan had recently passed away.

I stood up, on the brink of flooding the field with my tears, and snapped, 'Well, you don't have a nan. Your nan is *dead*.' I wheeled round and ran back to the school building, sobbing, angry, hurt, but also embarrassed about what I'd said to Cara.

When I got home from school, Mum was in her armchair, watching the TV. Instinctively, I went to her and climbed onto her lap. 'Please can I have a cuddle, Mummy?' I said.

I curled into Mum's stilted embrace. 'You're getting a bit too big to be sitting on my lap, really, Elizabeth,' she said. I dropped my face into my hands and burst into tears, Cara's comments spinning in my head: *You don't have real parents. Your* real *mum didn't want you, so she gave you away. Your mum isn't your* real *mum.* 'Goodness, Elizabeth, what on earth is the matter?'

Just then, the telephone in the hallway rang. Mum shifted me to one side. 'I'll need to get that,' she said. I stayed in a foetal position on the armchair, whimpering with jagged breaths. The drilling ring of the phone stopped, but I couldn't hear what Mum was saying over the blare of the TV. By the time she came back into the living room, I'd moved to my footstool, still catching my breath from crying so much. Mum returned to her armchair, her expression somewhere between displeased and puzzled. She sat on the edge of the chair, hands on her knees, regarding me for a few seconds. 'That was your teacher on the telephone,' she began, 'she said you've been teasing Cara about her grandmother dying. That doesn't sound like something you'd do, Elizabeth. Is this true? Did you tease Cara about her grandmother?'

I broke down again, my shoulders and chest trembling as fresh tears poured down my face. Traumatised by Cara's remarks, I'd forgotten the spiteful words I'd delivered in retaliation. Mum was right; it was unlike me to say hurtful things, and I knew what I'd said to Cara was awful, but in that desperate moment, I think I'd been trying to equate the feeling of loss in my mind: *my real parents didn't want me, but Cara's nan is dead.* My riposte had seemed my only defence at the time.

I inhaled sharply, then the words poured out of my mouth in one wobbly exhalation. 'Cara said my real mummy didn't want me and ...' I took another breath and continued, calmer now. 'She was teasing me about being adopted. She said you're not my real mummy – and that my *real* mummy gave me away. Other girls at school are teasing me too.'

Mum patted her thighs. 'Okay, come here,' she said.

I sat on her lap again for a few minutes and she said something like, 'What Cara said to you was nasty, but remember, Elizabeth, you haven't been brought up to say nasty things yourself.' I can't remember her exact words, but I do know that, as usual, there was no dialogue about my adoption. To give Mum her due, she did visit my teacher the next day to report the bullying.

Looking back on those days, remembering Mum's remark – 'You're getting a bit too big to be sitting on my lap, really, Elizabeth' – I realise I probably did act younger than my age then. But it's clear to me now: I craved cuddles from Mum because my body was yearning for my birth mother. My need for affection stemmed back to the preverbal trauma I had suffered as a baby.

The family tree experience hit me hard. It really prompted me to consider, *I call these people 'aunty', 'uncle', 'my cousins', 'nan', 'granddad', but they're not my blood relatives. I've been put in this family, but I feel like a stranger.*

There was one man who didn't appear on my family tree but who *was* real – to me. He was a kind, generous and cheery soul with boundless energy, who visited our house once a year. That man was Father Christmas.

I could rely on Father Christmas. Without fail, he turned up at our house every year on 24 December and, as we slept, he somehow came down our chimney, with his loaded sack, and left gifts for us.

Although I knew Father Christmas delivered presents to millions of children across the world on Christmas Eve, I always imagined, *he's here for me.* I thought he was so magical. The excitement that coursed through me on Christmas morning is still so memorable; I can feel it even now. Andrew and I would always wake up early, around 6.30 a.m., and charge downstairs to the lounge to find our two bright red cloth sacks full of presents – one labelled 'Elizabeth', the other, 'Andrew'. We'd jump up and down, squealing, 'He's been, he's been,' in unison, then we'd take our sacks up to Mum and Dad's room to open our gifts from Father Christmas. We were always extremely grateful for the lovely presents we received, but more than anything, I remember the warm, tingly glow I'd feel, knowing that Father Christmas had come, for *us*.

In December 1985, however, my festive 'reality' as I knew it was ruined. Again, a girl in my class upset me with another unbearable truth. During our morning break on the last day of term, I joined my friends, Sally and Chantelle, on a bench in the playground, our usual spot. We started chatting about Christmas and the kinds of presents we hoped to receive.

'I've asked for some new hair-crimpers,' said Sally, 'Among other stuff, of course.'

'Ha ha, I think I know all my presents already ... I found them in Mum and Dad's wardrobe. I've been peeking,' added Chantelle, giggling into her hand.

'Oh my God, that's *such* an obvious hiding place.' Sally's eyes shot skywards, then she looked at me. 'What about you, Elizabeth – do *you* know what you're getting?'

'Well,' I said, 'on my list to Father Christmas I did ask for some *Flower Fairies* books and some craft materials and some new—'

Sally and Chantelle's giggles rippled through my sentence, through the bench. 'Wait a minute,' said Chantelle, straight-faced now. 'You do know Father Christmas doesn't exist, don't you? That Father Christmas is your *parents* – *they* buy your presents?'

I fell silent for a few seconds, assimilating Chantelle's statement. I didn't want to appear silly in front of the girls – they were, after all, a year older than me. So, I got up, mumbled, 'Of course,' made some excuse about needing the loo, and walked away.

For the rest of the school day, I couldn't stop thinking about my earlier conversation with the girls. *Perhaps Chantelle was joking?* I hadn't questioned Father Christmas's existence until now.

As soon as I got home that afternoon, I decided to raise the matter with Mum. I went into the kitchen, where she was making a cup of tea. 'My friend Chantelle said Father Christmas isn't real. She says our parents buy our presents – but that isn't true, is it?' The desperation in my voice was clear.

I waited for Mum's incredulous look, for her to say Chantelle had it all wrong. Instead, she pulled a face that read 'busted' and spread her hands. 'Well, I suppose you'd find out sooner or later, Elizabeth,' she said. Then she filled the kettle.

I was devastated by Mum's reaction, upset that she hadn't tried harder to keep up the pretence. As for Father Christmas, I felt let down; he was just another lie, although I still clung to the hope that he existed. On Christmas Eve that year, I sat alone at my bedroom window, searching the sky for the glittering streak of his sleigh zooming overhead. I willed it to appear.

* * *

I've only recently realised that my reactions to certain situations as a child were trauma responses. I had no control of my environment and nobody to talk to about my feelings, which compounded my anxiety.

I think I developed obsessive-compulsive disorder. From an early age I couldn't fall asleep at bedtime. I had this routine that I called 'putting things straight'. Alone in my room at night, I'd switch on the lamp, get out of bed and flit around for ages, tidying. My doll's house had to be in its exact spot, under the basin by the bay window. I'd arrange my Body Shop toiletries – fruity soaps, bath oil pearls and shower gels – into groups of rainbow colours on the dressing table and make sure my books were in alphabetical order. If anything in my room was out of place, I'd feel unsettled. I couldn't sleep until I'd 'put everything straight'.

Sometimes I still couldn't sleep even after I'd obsessively organised my belongings, so I'd tiptoe along the landing to the toilet, lock myself in, and sit on the floor with my back pressed against the radiator (always on throughout the night), making roses out of the toilet paper, separating the ply, then tearing and folding the sheets into petals.

Putting things straight and making roses were my protection mechanisms, my very own form of avoidance. Fortunately, being creative proved a healthy distraction from my worries at times.

I adored making things. During the summer holidays, I'd watch the BBC programme *Why Don't You*. The show featured fun ideas to keep children occupied, from outdoor activities to cooking and arts and crafts projects, which I'd copy at home. I kept a box under my bed, packed with bits and bobs: ribbons I'd saved from presents, empty Quality Street wrappers, trays that had once held Ferrero Rocher chocolates, pipe cleaners and coloured pieces of paper. These were my precious craft materials. I'd spend hours sorting through my arty paraphernalia, marvelling at all the colours and textures and deciding what to create next. That box was my treasure trove of inspiration.

Sadly, Mum didn't share my passion for crafts; she didn't do creative activities with me, and I think this opened a wider chasm between us.

One afternoon, in spring 1986, I came home from school feeling enthused after making collages in art class. I had an idea for an ethereal *Flower Fairies*-inspired collage, composed from the sheets of pastel-coloured tissue paper I'd recently squirrelled away inside my art box. My noodle-thin pink and green ribbons would be perfect for this piece too. I thought, *I'll coil the ribbons into leaves and flowers and glue them over the tissue layers.*

I visualised my intended work as I dashed upstairs to my room, keen to get started. Kneeling on the carpet, I lifted the vallance on my bed and lowered my head, expecting to see my box in its usual spot. It wasn't there. All I saw beneath my bed was vacuumed carpet. Thinking the cleaner or Mum had moved it, I looked around my room, I checked inside my wardrobes, but my box was nowhere to be found.

I raced downstairs. Mum was in the hallway heading towards the living room, carrying a porcelain mug of tea. I stood on the bottom stair, clutching the banister. 'Where's my box gone?' I said.

Mum stopped, took a sip of her tea and said, 'Which box?'

'The one that was under my bed.'

Our cat, Tabitha, slinked into the hall, padding circles around Mum's feet. 'Oh, I threw that box out, Elizabeth,' she said, smiling down at Tabitha, who was now meowing and brushing her head against Mum's calf. 'It was full of rubbish.'

'That wasn't rubbish. Those were my art materials. I was going to make something.' I didn't even wait to hear Mum's response. I swung around and ran upstairs to my bedroom, slamming the door behind me. I sat beneath the bay window, my legs pulled up into my chest, forehead on my knees, and cried. Devastated that Mum had thrown out my art gear and didn't understand me. *She never did ... at all.*

Try as I might to connect with Mum, that bond simply wasn't there. We argued a lot at home and after these rows I'd shut myself in my room and cry. During those fiery episodes, I wanted to scream, 'You can't tell me what to do – you're not even my real mum. My real mum wouldn't treat me like this.' I never did say this, though, because I was frightened of the consequences. I feared Mum might decide she no longer wanted me as a daughter, that I wasn't behaving exactly how she liked, that I wasn't 'put straight'. Maybe she would send me away.

When you grow up as an adoptee, nobody prepares you. It's a societal conditioning that you should be grateful for your new 'family'. Nobody considers your abandonment, not really. No one stops to think how certain occasions or situations might trigger raw heartache.

My birthday is still a trigger point for me. I'm not alone; speaking to other adoptees, I have realised that they share this difficulty. But as far back as I can remember, I've felt a deep sadness on my birthday because I knew this was the one day of the year when my birth mother must surely think about me. I'd imagine, *Is she counting the years? Is she wondering what I look like, just as I'm constantly trying to picture her face?* But

I'd never allow my melancholy to show on my birthday. I smiled through my childhood parties at home, and I appreciated those parties, the presents, and people celebrating the day I arrived in this world. A day when neither my adoptive parents nor my extended family were actually present. A day they can tell me nothing about. They celebrated my birthday every single year, but never knew the day I came into this world – never even knew of my existence. Every year it hit me – the physicality of being born to my birth parents, yet having to pretend to celebrate being someone else's child was sometimes too much to bear for me.

Mother's Day has also always been a tough occasion for me. Mothering Sunday in our family was, naturally, all about Mum. On the Saturday beforehand, Dad would take Andrew and me to the shop to choose cards. A fog of confusion and helplessness enveloped me whenever I faced this task. I'd stare blankly at the rows of cards emblazoned with hearts and flowers and illustrations depicting perfect mother-daughter scenes. I'd see a woman in a long, flowing dress, holding her little girl's hand as they ambled through a sunlit meadow. Other cards declared in swirly calligraphy 'I love you, Mum' and 'Best Mum in the World' and other similar statements. They used to make me feel a bit sick. They still do. I was caught in a whirlwind of dilemmas: *Which card is appropriate for me to give? For our relationship? What words do I write inside the card? I don't quite know what to say. Has nobody considered how difficult this is for me, knowing that I have a real mother out there ... somewhere?* I felt trapped between conforming to the role of the dutiful, indebted daughter and honouring my own emotions towards this challenging day.

On Mother's Day morning, we'd all get dressed up and go to church. At the end of the service, the children would file over to a trestle table loaded with potted primulas and we'd each choose a plant to give to our mother. After church, the four of us would head to a restaurant for Sunday lunch. I'd play along with the merriment of the day, wishing Mum a happy Mother's Day, masking my sadness as once again, our parents didn't ask Andrew and me: 'How are you feeling? Is today difficult for you?' It was never, ever acknowledged – not on this day, not ever. I'd gaze around the room, consumed with silent thoughts about my real mother, looking at each blonde-haired, blue-eyed woman in turn, wondering, *Could that be her?*

My desire to see my birth mother's face grew stronger with age. How I wished I had even one photograph of her. Had my adoptive parents met her? If not, had they seen a picture of her? Then, one snowy January afternoon, soon after my thirteenth birthday, I began to fabricate a more vivid picture in my mind of what my birth mother *might* look like.

As I lay on my bed, reading, my hair scraped into a messy bun, Mum came in, cradling a pile of my freshly ironed clothes. Placing the bundle on the bed, she tilted her head and stared pensively at me for a few seconds. 'What's wrong?' I asked. I'd never seen her look at me this intensely.

'Nothing's wrong, Elizabeth. I was just thinking, you're very pretty. You remind me of Grace Kelly, actually.'

I sat up, intrigued, and surprised that she was able to connect my features to another human being. 'Who's Grace Kelly?'

'Oh, Grace Kelly was a glamorous American film star,' said Mum. 'She was married to a prince.'

'Wow, a film star ... married to a prince?' This was a real-life fairy tale. My mind raced. *Maybe my birth mother is famous. Is she a film star, royalty even? Perhaps that's why she couldn't keep me – because she was too famous to reveal her secret ... me.*

'That's right. Although unfortunately, Grace Kelly was killed in a car crash a few years ago.' Mum hugged her upper arms. 'Brrr, it's cold in here,' she muttered on her way out.

Her words hung in the room. She had just told me I reminded her of somebody, a real person out there, beyond my reflection in the bathroom mirror.

Obviously, there was no internet back then, so I couldn't Google pictures of Grace Kelly, but after the weekend, I looked her up in the school library. I found a picture of Grace in a book about Hollywood movie stars. Sitting alone in a quiet corner of the library, I pored over this photograph. Mum's observation stood out; I noticed I did resemble the actress in some ways – we both had blonde hair and blue eyes, the same peaches-and-cream complexion. I lightly stroked her face on the page, tears welling in my eyes. Grace's smile radiated gentleness. 'Is this what you look like? Are you a princess? A film star?' I whispered.

I stayed in the library for quite a while, staring at the picture, crying and smiling at the same time.

When I got home, I went back into the bathroom, shut the door and stared into the mirror again, this time discovering warmth, kindness, something much more special than before. I'd never considered that I could mirror somebody else beyond my physical features. *Maybe my birth mother had a pure heart. Maybe she had deep thoughts and an understated smile for the outside world, just like me.*

I smiled at my reflection and decided, *One day, I'm going to have a beautiful baby daughter myself. I'll love her with all my heart. I'll never, ever, ever let her go ... and I'm going to name her Grace.*

3

Who's Claire?

Andrew's prep school, Worcestershire, Sunday, 4 October 1987
I twisted around in the back seat of the car, staring through the rear window at Andrew as we pulled away from the boarding school Mum and Dad had sent him to in September.

My brother had been home for a weekend exeat, one that had flown by too quickly – and now we were leaving him, tiny and alone before the grand Edwardian building, blushed in the afternoon autumn sun.

Seconds ago, I'd hugged and kissed my brother goodbye. I'd squeezed him tight in my arms, not wanting to let him go. 'I'll miss you,' I'd told him, trying to fathom why we were being separated.

I waved slowly from behind the glass, Andrew diminishing to the size of a Lego figure as we advanced down the drive edged with old, golden trees that had seen so much. Loneliness ached in my heart and wrenched my stomach.

Mum whimpered from the passenger seat, 'I miss him already. My good, sweet boy.' Andrew had always been the golden child in our home, the compliant one who obeyed the rules. Unlike me, he didn't ask Mum and Dad about his birth parents. Mum deemed me 'difficult' and 'problematic', which I never understood. I wasn't troublesome; I was just headstrong, inquisitive, and deeply tormented within myself.

Andrew became smaller and smaller as we reached the end of the long drive. We turned left, and my brother vanished. I sat silently, watching the countryside streak past in a blur of russet tones.

I'm on my own again.

Mum and Dad had decided to send Andrew to a new prep school at the end of the last school term. I think they felt he wasn't fulfilling his potential at his prep school in Edgbaston, which was just down the road from my school. His new prep school, with its prestigious reputation would give him better opportunities, they said.

Andrew, my little buddy, had gone and it was just Mum, Dad, me, and our new ginger kittens, Tom and Jessie, in the house. (Tabitha had died while we were on holiday in the Canary Islands. Our neighbours, Bob and Vanessa, who had been feeding Tabitha in our absence, found her limp body in our hallway one morning.)

I missed Andrew terribly. I felt like an only child at home. Andrew and I shouldn't have been split up. I thought we were in this together – you can't build a relationship with a sibling if you're separated. Loss is a pertinent feature to an adoptee, and I felt I had just lost my little brother. I'd sit alone at the kitchen table, drawing versions of my pretty cottage scene or at my bedroom window, watching the roses bloom, wilt and die as the seasons changed, longing for Andrew to come home. Wishing we could go out on our bikes, play a game or even do our cleaning chores together, when we'd giggle behind Mum's back at the silliness of picking 'bits' out of the maroon carpet.

Things didn't get much better for me at school either. As Andrew settled into his new home thirty-five miles away in the Malvern Hills, I suffered another bullying episode in the playground in Edgbaston.

Sian was one of the cool girls in my year. She had long, permed hair – Mum would never let me perm *or* colour my hair, even if I had wanted to – and a worldly air. When Sian spoke, other girls listened, as they did on this occasion when she targeted me.

I was among a small cluster of girls, including Sian, chatting in the playground that lunchtime. I can't even recall what we were talking about before Sian started on me. Her words came from nowhere in a voice loaded with malice. Sian's curls, locked in a banana clip, danced as she spoke. She stabbed her index finger at me, her stare burning holes through me. 'You're a bastard,' she said. A sniggering chorus of approval erupted, and Sian's face broke into a satisfied smile. 'That's what you are, Elizabeth – a bastard.'

I shrunk inside my blazer, feeling my face glowing red. *What's a bastard?* I didn't know what those two guttural syllables meant, but they sounded bad. *Is bastard a swear word?*

'I'm a *what?*' I asked.

Sian arched her eyebrows. 'A *bastard*,' she repeated.

I stepped backwards as that final 'd' punched me in the stomach. Humiliated and confused, I walked away, around the corner of the school building, where I spotted one of my favourite teachers, Mrs Fellows-Smith, who was on playground duty. I approached my teacher and asked her outright, 'What's a bastard?'

Mrs Fellows-Smith drew a sharp breath. 'Goodness, Elizabeth. That's a swear word. Where have you heard that?'

'One of the girls just said to me, "You're a bastard",' I replied. 'I know it's a bad word because it *sound*s horrible, but I don't know what it means. What does it mean?'

'Oh, erm, it, well …' Mrs Fellows-Smith floundered for a moment, the conversation clearly awkward for her. 'Well, Elizabeth, you're right,' she said finally. 'It *is* a horrible, offensive word for a baby whose parents aren't married.' She sealed that sentence with a sympathetic smile. 'That was a nasty thing for you to hear from another girl, but I'm sure she didn't mean it. She was probably just being silly, that's all. Now, why don't you go and find some other girls to play with.'

I felt disappointed that Mrs Fellows-Smith hadn't asked who had labelled me a 'bastard'. Sian had hurt and embarrassed me in front of my friends – friends who had laughed along at my expense. I couldn't shake the word from my mind. I didn't find 'other girls to play with' either, I was mortified. Instead, I hurried inside, tears stinging my eyes. I needed to be alone, so I spent the rest of the lunch hour inside a toilet cubicle, sobbing. *I'm a bastard*, I thought. *My real parents weren't married so I'm a bastard, even though my adoptive parents* are *married.*

When I relayed the 'bastard' event to Mum, she reported it to the school, as she did after Cara told me, 'Your real parents didn't want you.' I looked 'bastard' up in the dictionary, which informed me, as Mrs Fellows-Smith had explained, that the word means 'person born of unmarried parents; an illegitimate child'. *How could Sian have said such a wicked thing to me?* After Mum called the school, the matter appeared to be done and dusted. Nobody called me 'bastard' again. Everyone moved on. Except me.

Even in my teens, I was naïve in some respects. Maybe I should've known the meaning of the word 'bastard' by then, but my parents sheltered me from so much at home. They didn't talk about these issues or any other subjects they considered uncomfortable. Mum never gave me the birds and the bees talk; everything I knew about reproduction I'd learned from the dated book that lived inside the kitchen drawer – Margaret Sheffield's *Where Do Babies Come From?* – and sex education classes at school. Although I do recall Mum awkwardly trying to explain periods to me when I was around ten.

We were in the car one day, heading back from the weekly supermarket shop, when Mum suddenly asked, 'Do you know what a period is, Elizabeth?'

'Of course, a period is an era, like in history,' I replied from the back seat.

'Well, that's correct, but it also means something else. It's something that happens when you become a woman.'

I leaned forward, eager to hear more. Mum didn't even look at me in the rear-view mirror as she spoke hurriedly about how I'd 'bleed down below' once a month. 'It'll probably start when you're twelve or thirteen.' Next, Mum mumbled something about how periods 'prepare women's bodies for pregnancy' before swiftly diverting the conversation to my upcoming piano exam.

Naturally, when my first period arrived, aged fourteen, I thought about my birth mother. *Was she the same age when she started her periods? How did she feel when she found out she was pregnant with me? Angry? Sad? Frightened? Was there a chance she'd wanted to keep me but wasn't allowed to – because she was unmarried?* My adoptive parents said my birth mother was 'young' when she had me. How young was she? A teenager perhaps? I still saw her as Grace Kelly – that image was all I had to go on. I still dreamed about having a baby of my own one day. In my head, that child was always a girl, my baby Grace.

Like most teenagers, I argued with my parents – mostly with Mum – but there was a deeper current surging through my angst. After every row I'd ask myself the same questions: *Why am I in this family? What did I do wrong as an innocent,*

49

newborn baby for my mother to give me away? Who am I?
There were no answers for me, no rationalising, and the weight
of my insecurities engulfed me. I knew my birth certificate and
adoption papers were locked inside a filing cabinet in the study.
Every time I went in there, I'd look at the silver keyhole in the
cabinet's drawer, wondering what secrets from my past were
hidden behind it.

I constantly asked Mum and Dad if I could see my adoption
papers, which invariably made them bristle. They'd exchange
awkward looks and say, 'Maybe when you're older, Elizabeth.'
Or they'd change the subject. Part of me understood their
responses, because I knew that my questions must've been
difficult for them to hear and answer, but for some reason, they
didn't want me to know my story, which only intensified my
curiosity. *Who am I?*

It didn't help that I was at the age when I wanted to explore
my individuality and style, but this too was cramped by Mum.
I told her I wanted to be known as 'Liz'; my closest friends
shortened my name and I really liked it. I felt more like a 'Liz'
than an 'Elizabeth', which sounded so formal. Even Bob next
door called me 'Lizzie'. But no, Mum insisted, 'You're not Liz,
you're Elizabeth. I gave you that name.' I wanted to *claim* my
name. I wanted to be me, yet I still didn't know who the real
me was. My life felt like an interminable anxiety dream of
uncertainty and frustration.

Whenever Mum took me clothes shopping, I'd gravitate
towards denim jackets, leggings and Doc Marten boots,
and she'd tut her disapproval and steer me towards more
conservative dresses, with frills and collars – the kinds of things
she might have dressed me in four years previously. In the shoe
department, she'd choose yet another pair of prim Mary Janes

for me. She still wanted to dress me, to control me. I had no say in the matter. I felt utterly stifled.

Mum did notice my creative talents. Occasionally, she'd let me do her make-up before she and Dad went to one of their functions. I loved doing this, and I think Mum was impressed by my skills, despite her usual comment of, 'I just need to blend this a bit more' when I'd finished.

It was as though Mum wanted me to stay a young child forever. So, naturally, she wasn't happy when I got my first boyfriend, at the age of fourteen.

I thought Mum would approve of Nathan, whose mother was a religious education teacher – at my school even. There wasn't anything to dislike about him. Nathan was polite, softly spoken, caring, and angelically handsome with turquoise eyes and a mop of very blond hair. My relationship with Nathan was innocent; we'd chat on the telephone and meet up occasionally at the weekends. It was all just 'nice'. We only ever shared a few kisses.

I enjoyed having a boyfriend. Nathan liked me, he made me feel wanted and special and I cherished spending time with him – when I was allowed to.

Just before Christmas 1988, he gave me two gifts, both beautifully wrapped in gold foil and lush red satin ribbons. 'Go on, open them,' he urged, eyes twinkling with excitement.

'This is so sweet of you,' I said, gently untying the bow on a soft, flat rectangular present. I was moved by Nathan's kindness, and gasped when I peeled back the paper to reveal a stunning navy blue lambswool scarf, which I immediately put on. 'This is beautiful,' I gushed, stroking the soft fabric, 'thank you so much.'

The second present was a bottle of White Musk perfume from the Body Shop. 'I remember you saying you love Body

Shop stuff,' said Nathan as I sprayed my wrists and inhaled the scent of lily-of-the-valley, jasmine and musk.

I threw my arms around Nathan and thanked him again. 'Oh, I love this perfume.' That was a precious moment for me; I felt lucky to have such a thoughtful boyfriend. Little did I know my happiness would soon be sabotaged.

Mum made it clear from the outset that she disapproved of my having a boyfriend. I wasn't allowed to be alone with Nathan in my bedroom. 'No going upstairs with him. You're too young for that,' Mum would say. So, we'd have to sit in the lounge, or at the kitchen table, as if we were about to start our homework, Mum giving Nathan judgemental looks whenever she walked past us, which was often. We had no privacy; Mum obviously feared we might get up to mischief, even at that tender age. Maybe she thought I might have sex with Nathan and end up pregnant. Imagine the shame if that were to happen. What would the neighbours think? What would The Gang say? She needn't have worried, though.

Nathan had been my boyfriend for a few weeks when Mum decided enough was enough. Early one Saturday morning, the house phone rang. Expecting a call from Nathan – we were hoping to see each other later that day – I bolted from my bedroom, down the stairs. Unfortunately, Mum beat me to the phone. 'No, that won't be happening,' she said firmly into the receiver. 'We're not allowing Elizabeth to have boyfriends … she's too young. Don't call again. Goodbye.' Mum calmly returned the receiver to its cradle with a devastating soft clunk.

'Mum, why did you …' I couldn't find the words. She'd told my first ever boyfriend, the person who meant the world to me, that our relationship was over.

'Have you got your books together for your piano lesson, Elizabeth?' was Mum's response.

I wasn't allowed to see Nathan after that phone call. I was heartbroken; first, I'd lost my brother, now I'd lost my boyfriend. I saw Nathan as someone who had actively chosen to be with me, for me. But Mum had taken that away from me, destroyed it, without explanation, without warning. I was livid at the control she exercised over me.

A year passed before I met my next boyfriend. I'd just started in the lower sixth at school, studying for A-levels in French, history and music. Like Nathan, Mark went to the boys' school, but he was a bit older than me. Tall and funny, with brown, floppy hair, I fell for Mark in a big, tummy-flipping way. Mum didn't like him. 'He's on drugs,' she once commented, although I've no idea how she came to that conclusion. I certainly hadn't seen any evidence that Mark was taking drugs of any description.

Mostly, I met Mark at his house, but my regimental regime at home curtailed our relationship somewhat. I always had to be home by a certain time; Mark rarely came to our house because I still wasn't allowed boys in my bedroom. Mum's strictness bothered Mark. 'Blimey, your mum won't let you do anything, will she?' he'd often remark.

Being an older-looking seventeen-year-old, Mark had no trouble getting served in pubs. He was always suggesting we should go to a bar together. 'Sorry, I can't,' I had to tell him. 'Mum and Dad would kill me if they knew I'd been to a pub.' Mark would roll his eyes at that.

Still, I naïvely thought Mark and I were strong; I assumed, after two months together, that this might be a long-term relationship. I got this horribly wrong.

I'd arranged to meet Mark at his house one afternoon, but he wasn't there when I arrived. His mum made me a cup of tea and showed me into the lounge. 'He shouldn't be long,' she said, gesturing at the television cabinet. 'You can watch a video while you wait.' I put on the Guns N' Roses concert video that Mark and I had watched several times before (we both loved Guns N' Roses), drank my tea and waited, patiently at first. After half an hour, I grew tetchy. I had no clue where Mark had gone – we didn't have mobile phones back then so I couldn't call or text him. *He'd invited me here, so where was he?*

Mark eventually turned up about ten minutes later, as Axl Rose screeched the opening lines of 'Welcome to the Jungle'. He shambled into the lounge and sat next to me on the sofa, raking his hands through his hair. 'Where have you been?' I asked him.

Mark dropped his hands into his lap with a sigh. 'I was in the pub.'

'But you told me to meet you here. I've been waiting for you.'

A pause, filled with dense guitar riffs. 'Look, there's something I need to tell you,' he said, shifting to face me.

'What? What's wrong?'

'I don't think we should see each other any more, Liz. It's not … working out, is it?'

My skin prickled with panic, exacerbated by the strident strains of 'Welcome to the Jungle' – a track Mark and I had once happily sung along to, but now it had become our break-up song. 'But … why?'

Mark shrugged. 'Look, I'm sorry, but you're not allowed to do anything. I'm not allowed in your bedroom. You're not allowed to go certain places. It's your mother. She doesn't let us do *anything*. She's a dragon. I think we should split up.'

The room turned misty through my tears. I was angry at Mark, angry at Mum, angry at the world. 'I need to call my dad,' I choked. 'I'll get him to pick me up.'

I cried all the way home in the car. 'Cheer up, Elizabeth,' said Dad. 'Plenty more fish in the sea.'

That evening, I lay on the sofa in the living room, sobbing my eyes out while Mum and Dad sat in their armchairs, watching television. I was completely distraught, broken. All I wanted was for my parents to get out of their chairs and give me a hug.

It took me several weeks to get over my break-up with Mark, to try to understand why he'd abandoned me so suddenly, examining all the ifs and whys surrounding the situation. *If Mum was different, would Mark and I still be together? Would Mum's overbearing ways damage my future relationships? If he loved me, surely, he'd endure Mum for my sake. Why did he hurt me?*

* * *

Career-wise, I was unsure what I wanted to do. For a while, I dreamed of becoming a beauty journalist, inspired by the elegant sales assistants I'd admired as a child in Rackhams perfumery department, the articles in the teen magazines I loved to read and my ever-present fantasy of glamorous Grace Kelly. When I mentioned this idea to Mum, she pooh-poohed it with a scowl. 'Oh, you don't want to be a beauty journalist, Elizabeth,' she said. 'There's no money in *that*.'

I thought I was doing well in the lower sixth, juggling three A-levels at fifteen alongside all the chaos that raged inside my head. Then around the time of my predicted grades, a few months after my sixteenth birthday, Mum and Dad dropped a bombshell – in the lounge, of course.

They returned home from my school's parents' evening with serious, concerned faces. I'd been excited to hear what my teachers had said about me; I always worked hard and usually handed my assignments in on time. We assumed our usual triangle formation – Mum in her armchair next to the fire, Dad in his seat beside his mahogany stereo cabinet, while I sat on the footstool.

'Your teachers said you'll have to make some drastic changes if you're to achieve respectable A-level grades, Elizabeth,' said Dad. 'They feel you could do much better.'

'What? But I've been working hard.'

Dad glanced at Mum, then cleared his throat. 'The thought is that you should repeat the year. You can do the lower sixth again. That way, you'll be able to catch up and get the grades that you deserve.'

That news hit me like a bullet. 'No way,' I cried. To repeat the lower sixth, with the girls in the year below me ... I couldn't bear the shame. 'I don't want to repeat the year. I'll work harder. I'll even—'

'Sorry, Elizabeth, but we feel this is for the best. Your teachers think it's for the best and—'

'Well, there is another idea,' Mum interjected. 'You could go away to boarding school, like Andrew. You could start sixth form again there.'

Her words seemed to echo for a moment as I assimilated the possibility of leaving here, starting again. The potential freedom of boarding school began to settle in my mind, replacing my horror in a split second. This was the best idea ever to escape Mum's lips. My going away to school would give me a fresh start. My classmates would be the same age as me, they wouldn't need to know I was repeating the lower sixth. I replied quickly. 'Yes, I think boarding school would be a much better option for me.'

Mum nodded slowly and squinted at her watch; *Emmerdale* was about to start. 'Okay, that's what we'll do then. We'll start looking at possible schools for you, Elizabeth.' I wanted to do a little dance around the lounge, cheer at the top of my voice, but I knew this wouldn't go down well, so I waited until I was inside my bedroom, then I punched the air and exclaimed, 'Yes.'

The following week, we visited three schools. In the end, we chose Malvern Girls' College, housed in a beautiful old building opposite the quaint railway station of Great Malvern. I couldn't wait to start. Come September, I'd be free. I'd be close to Andrew again and, hopefully, I'd discover what it meant to be 'me'.

Before my new adventure began, however, I had to finish the school year at Edgbaston Church of England College for Girls. During this time, I continued to ask my parents to show me my adoption documents. 'I'm sixteen now – I'm old enough to know the truth,' I persisted. Until one day, they finally relented. Perhaps it was because I was going away that they decided I was *ready*.

I'll never forget the evening that Mum and Dad presented my papers to me. As per tradition, this was another monumental event in the lounge, in our same triangular seating arrangement. I can still smell the musty aroma of the old typewriter paper that held the secrets of my beginnings.

My file was surprisingly thick, containing around twenty-five sheets of A4 paper. I read my original birth certificate first, the clocks ticking tensely with my heart as I tried to process the information before me. According to my certificate, I was born at Barratt Maternity Home in Northampton. My birth date was there, in vintage-looking joined up writing – *Eleventh January 1974*. Written in a box below headed, *Name and Surname,* were the words *Claire Elaine Watts*. I looked up at Mum and Dad. 'Who's *Claire?*' I asked. 'Who's Claire Elaine Watts?'

Mum's mouth twitched. 'That's you.'

'Me? How can it be me?' I couldn't believe it. *I'm not Claire, I'm Liz.*

'That's the name you were given at birth. We changed your name when we adopted you,' Dad explained.

I continued reading, still in a state of shock. Claire? There were several Claires at my school. *I don't look or act like them.* A line filled the box titled *FATHER,* but my birth mother's name was there: *Yvonne Shirley WATTS (a clerk). Place of birth: Romford, Essex.*

I tried to mouth 'Yvonne', but my bottom lip stuck in the grip of my top teeth with my silent 'v'. I reread her name, then my eyes fell on her signature – Y. S. Watts, small and neat, the two t's in 'Watts' fused by a single cross. It felt surreal. I thought, *This is* her. *This is my birth mother. She signed this document – this is her handwriting. After all these years, I have a name for my mother.*

My entrance into this world was registered on 15 January 1974. The word 'Adopted' glared at me from the page.

I turned to the next document titled 'Summary for Adoption and Care Committee', dated 13 February 1974 and written by a care worker assigned to Yvonne by the Barratt Maternity Home. Mum and Dad didn't say a word. They remained in their armchairs, still as the Royal Doulton ladies on the coffee table.

The summary was tough to digest, too much to take in, particularly the opening passage labelled 'Mother'. The first line confirmed Yvonne's date of birth as 6 January 1954 and her nationality: *British, nominally Church of England.* The next few lines hurt me to the core:

> Yvonne told me that she had wanted an abortion but had been
> refused on the grounds of insufficient reason for it. She had not
> told her parents about the pregnancy although she was living

with them, until after the refusal of the abortion, and she said they took it quite well.

Yvonne is an only child, and having discussed the situation with her parents, has decided on adoption as the best course.

During her pregnancy Yvonne was not particularly well; she seemed to have a series of minor indispositions with frequent colds and coughs. However, the pregnancy itself was uneventful and the delivery normal.

I couldn't speak; my mouth and throat were bone-dry. How was I supposed to process this information? My birth mother had wanted an abortion. *She didn't want me.* The care worker inferred Yvonne's parents were fine with her pregnancy – then when her abortion was 'refused', on the grounds of *insufficient reason for it,* she decided to give me away. *I wouldn't be here now, reading this, if Yvonne* had *aborted me.*

Halfway down the page, two underlined words read, *Putative Father.* My alleged father's name was Andrew Paul Conant, born 19 January 1955, the report told me. My mind ached with constant questions. *Did Yvonne not know who my birth father is? Is Andrew Conant my birth father? If he isn't my father, then who is? Why didn't Yvonne want to keep me?*

Reading on, it seemed likely that Andrew Conant was my birth father. As the care worker noted about the 'putative' father:

He had wished to bring up the baby; he and his fiancée (he had been engaged to another girl since July who is divorced and has a child of three) were hoping to marry and would like to take the baby.

I thought, *Why would Andrew Conant want to take me if he wasn't my father?* But reading on, I noticed he'd changed his mind soon after: *When I saw Andrew on the 1st February he agreed that adoption would be the best thing for the baby, as he had not yet married and it would be most impracticable to consider the course of action he had previously suggested.*

So, my birth father – if he *was* my birth father – didn't want to keep me either. I can't begin to explain how excruciatingly painful all of this was for me – how difficult it was, as a sixteen-year-old, to absorb these facts. I knew I'd never feel the same again after seeing my adoption file.

The final section of the 'Summary for Adoption and Care Committee' was marked *Baby*. I flinched when I saw the name Claire Elaine Watts again. I simply couldn't conceive that she was me. Claire Watts weighed 6 lbs 8 ozs at birth. She was discharged from the Barratt Maternity Home and passed to a foster mother in Northampton on 21 January 1974. *Who looked after me for ten days following my 'normal delivery'? Yvonne? Nurses?*

The baby is progressing very satisfactorily, observed the care worker, *eating and sleeping well. She is a nice compact baby with fair hair and complexion. Hair now going auburn, small red birthmark appearing on her right hip.*

A 'compact' baby. That description sounded odd to me – and I'd never noticed a birthmark on my right hip. I also wondered why Yvonne had given me a name, when she didn't intend to keep me.

I still had several documents to get through, more to learn about how and why I ended up here, in this house in Harborne, with parents who 'chose' me (many of us adoptees are told this 'chosen' story, yet the fact was that many of us were literally just the next available baby). *But who was I?* The answer was staring me in the face, there in black and white, yet I didn't recognise myself in the text. I raised my head and the room swayed slightly. Mum and Dad's features knotted into expressions that screamed, *This is difficult*. They knew the content I'd just read, but I didn't feel that they fully understood the weight of what I had just discovered.

The clocks chimed, declaring 7 p.m. For once, the TV was switched off. I waited for the chimes to end, then I asked my adoptive parents, asked myself, again, 'Who's Claire?'

4

Beginnings

I sat for ages reading my adoption file, my emotions racing from shock to anger, disbelief and heartache with every revelation.

The papers contained more details about Yvonne and Andrew's appearances and lives. I read that Yvonne was a 'neat', 'slightly built' woman, 'quite attractive', of medium height with fair straight hair and a 'pale, oval face'. One file submitted to the Adoption and Care Committee described Yvonne as 'pleasant, helpful and articulate' and included her hobbies: swimming, reading and knitting.

I learned that Yvonne had left school – a comprehensive in Billericay, Essex – at fifteen, and her family moved to Northampton in 1972. Before she fell pregnant with me at nineteen, she worked as a clerical assistant for the Express Lift Company in Northampton. The documents said she'd returned to live with her parents after my birth, with one passage contradicting what I'd previously seen concerning Yvonne's parents' reaction to her pregnancy. The following lines suggested to me that her father *wasn't* okay with her situation: *Her father was very belligerent about the putative father, saying he should contribute towards the fostering fees. Yvonne says she finds her father rather hard and unsympathetic, but she has quite a good relationship with her mother.*

It also dawned on me as I read this: *I have biological grandparents, too.* I wondered whether they were alive. *Is Yvonne alive? Would anybody inform us if something had happened to her?* I felt so overwhelmed, upset, unwanted and unloved, but equally, I *had* to know every detail logged in those yellowing pages. I'd waited and badgered my adoptive parents for so many years for this moment, to discover the truth behind my bloodline.

My 'putative' father, Andrew Conant, was five foot ten, well-built and had light brown hair and a fair complexion. He came from a broken home and, like Yvonne, was an only child. Born in Portsmouth, he spent three years in Kenya before moving to Northampton aged six. Andrew's parents separated shortly after they returned to the UK due to his father's 'drinking habits'. Andrew hadn't seen or spoken to his father in eight years and his mother, a cashier, had remarried.

I searched the text for clues that Andrew *was* my real father, but the only traits linking him with me were his fair complexion and apparent interest in animals. *He keeps tropical fish,* I read.

Andrew didn't like school, so he left at fifteen, ahead of his GCEs, and joined the Royal Navy for two years. At the time of my birth, he'd landed a job as a radio controller for the fire brigade. He liked all sports, especially rugby, my papers informed me.

On 1 February 1974, Andrew signed a form confirming he was the 'alleged father of Claire Watts' and that he had no objection to her 'being placed for adoption'.

I spent 52 days with a foster mother before the Church of England Children's Society 'introduced' me to my adoptive parents in a Northamptonshire diocesan office on 14 March 1974. They took me home the same day. Yvonne didn't want me, so, at ten days old, somebody wrapped me in a blanket and delivered me to a woman who looked after me for almost two months. My foster 'mother' presumably fed and dressed me before the Church of England Children's Society people took me away. Then, in an office I pictured as grey and soulless, I was handed to two more strangers who would soon become my 'parents'. It sounded like a warped game of pass the parcel to me, the prize being a vulnerable baby. *Did I scream for my birth mother during the drive from Northampton to Harborne? How did Yvonne feel when she let me go? Did she cry? Had Yvonne held me as a newborn? If so, why hadn't she fallen in love with her daughter, her baby Claire? Did her heart break when, on 7 May 1974, she signed the Birmingham County Court adoption order, relinquishing her parental rights?*

Does Yvonne regret her decision now?

A social worker visited me a few times during those first few weeks in Harborne to monitor how I was settling in. Reports said Mum and Dad were 'thrilled' and accepted me 'without hesitation'.

Another report stated that I was a 'very attractive child' with fair skin and auburn hair and, according to the social worker, this made me a 'good match' for my parents – because Mum too had 'auburn' hair and Dad 'was red-haired in his youth'. What a strange, irrelevant observation, written as if to say, *Ooh, how convenient – the baby has the same colour hair as her prospective parents. People might think she's their real child. Off you go, happy family.*

My adoption was legalised on 20 June 1974 at Birmingham County Court. A deep sadness consumed me as I reached the final A4 sheets that charted the first six months of my life, especially when I looked at my 'certified copy of an entry' in the Adopted Children Register – as *Elizabeth*. I knew this to be my legal document, rather than my original birth certificate. There was no mention of Claire Elaine Watts on this piece of paper. She had vanished. It was as though she'd never existed.

Skimming the earlier pages again, I still couldn't compute that Claire Elaine Watts was me, that Yvonne had wanted an abortion, or how I was passed around as a baby before finally being 'matched' to Mum and Dad. There was no going back. For me, the raw facts contained in my folder dismantled the pretence in our adoptive family unit.

Once I'd finished looking at the pages of my past, Mum and Dad locked them away again. I can't remember them saying much, other than, 'We'll photocopy these papers for you.' Their attitude was very much, *Oh well, we've given you what you wanted. Moving on.* Their pretence continued, but I barely slept that night. I remember climbing into my bed, curling up into a ball and sobbing. I felt utterly traumatised. From that moment on, I was broken.

I had to face up to what I'd learned about Yvonne, my 'putative' father and my adoption, but this would take me weeks, months, years to try to process. There was no 'support' for me as I went through this – no counselling, no check-ins to see how I was dealing with it all. I was on my own.

During the weeks after seeing my papers, the voice in my head tormented me, trying to piece the information together, to make sense of it all. I questioned the validity of the information contained in my papers. *Had Yvonne really wanted an abortion? Was Andrew Conant my real father? Had Yvonne given me away because her father disapproved of her pregnancy?* I wondered, as I had done for years, where my birth mother was now. *Was she thinking about me?* I scrutinised my right hip, searching for the birthmark noted by the care worker in my file. Nothing. *Did it ever exist? Or was it erased alongside my identity as Claire Elaine Watts?* I felt I'd lost the branding Yvonne had brought me into the world with. *Where was it? Where was Claire Elaine Watts?* I asked myself once again, *Why did she give me a name if she knew she wasn't going to keep me?* The truth was, only Yvonne could answer these questions, but I could only ask her if I could find her. But how? Who could help me find my birth mother? I had nobody to talk to, nobody to comfort me as I faced these agonising issues, but I did decide that one day I would like to find Yvonne. *Maybe I'll start looking for her once I've turned eighteen. Mum and Dad can't stand in my way once I'm legally an adult.*

* * *

I did, however, have something to look forward to: a new beginning – a fresh start in Malvern, away from the constraints of my adoptive home. Soon, my last day at Edgbaston Church of England College for Girls arrived. I said a teary farewell to my friends and teachers – bullying episodes aside, I had made some lovely friends – and walked away from the school I'd known since I was three.

The summer holidays couldn't pass quickly enough for me. I was excited to start at Malvern Girls' College and explore my identity. This began when Dad took me shopping for my new school shoes.

Dad never took me shoe or clothes shopping, it was always Mum in control of all that, but on this occasion, he did. It was about a week before the new term started, and I found a pair of black lace-up Doc Martens-style shoes. 'These are nice,' I said, picking up a shoe in my size.

Dad nodded. 'Yes, they look like good, sturdy, sensible shoes to me. I think your mother will approve.'

I tried on the shoes; they fitted perfectly and looked amazing. Dad agreed. 'Okay, we'll take them,' he said to the shop assistant. I felt so liberated to have picked something for myself

– even though I knew Mum would absolutely disapprove of my choice.

Indeed, Mum was horrified when she saw my shoes. She glared at Dad as though he were a stranger who'd barged into her house. 'Why have you bought her those big, chunky horrible shoes?' she demanded.

Dad shrugged. 'What?'

Thankfully, Mum didn't tell Dad to return my shoes, which I buried inside the suitcase that I took to Malvern the following Sunday.

I immediately fell in love with my new surroundings. The Malvern Hills, tranquil yet magnificent, filled me with a sense of calmness and creativity. Sir Edward Elgar was born in Malvern, and many of his great works, including the *Enigma Variations*, were inspired by the atmospheric beauty of the Malvern Hills. 'Nimrod', my favourite Enigma movement, played in my head as I marvelled at the spectacular views out of my dormitory and classroom windows.

The girls at Malvern were a lovely crowd and I soon settled in and made new friends. It was overwhelming at first, starkly different from my home in Harborne, where my parents' control had become my normality, an unwelcome security blanket. Although there were rules at Malvern Girls' School, I had some freedom to be myself, which felt like a big step forward. Within a few months, I began to feel like my own person. I shared a dormitory with three other girls – Fenella, Trudy and Karen – and we'd often sit up after lights out, giggling and chatting. It was like being at a sleepover every night. I loved that.

I tried to forget about my past at boarding school. I didn't tell my classmates about my adoption because I wanted a fresh start as me, *Liz*.

Away from Mum's watchful eye, I revelled in activities that would've landed me in big trouble at home. I got myself into a spot of bother during my first week at Malvern when the headmaster of the boys' school caught me smoking in the quaint café at the railway station opposite the school. I was mortified. (I'd secretly started smoking at fifteen; my neighbour Jess would come with me to buy a packet of Marlboro Lights cigarettes, then we'd walk around the block and hide in the big trees in the park so that I could smoke.)

The headmaster reported my smoking to my housemistress, and she gated me for two days. This didn't deter me from smoking back then, although I did quit the habit about twelve years later.

There was no uniform as such at school, but we had to dress formally in a dark suit, with a respectable length skirt during the week. At weekends, I'd experiment with fashions. I went through a tame goth-grunge stage, wearing black eye make-up, ripped jeans and oversized shirts. I remember buying an oversized German army shirt from an alternative clothes shop in the town centre.

One evening, I decided I wanted a second piercing in my right ear, so I asked my friend Fenella to do it with a needle in our dormitory. That was silly of me. I howled with pain as Fenella pushed the pin through my earlobe, sending a trickle of blood down the side of my neck.

My short-lived goth-grunge phase and piercing a second hole in my ear were my means of expression – a welcome diversion from the Elizabeth whom Mum and Dad had moulded in Harborne. At Malvern, my teachers and friends called me Liz, but Mum refused to accept my young adult identity. She'd call the communal house phone, and whenever one of my friends picked up a call, Mum would say, 'Is Elizabeth there?'

This threw my friends in my early days at Malvern. 'There isn't an Elizabeth here. Do you mean Liz?' they'd ask Mum. Yet still my adoptive mother wouldn't bend on my name. In her eyes, I would always be Elizabeth.

I didn't get homesick. I missed our cats, but I certainly didn't miss the tension that pervaded my adoptive family. My grades improved, too. I was now studying for a fourth A-level, general studies, in addition to French, history and music, alongside piano and oboe lessons. Musically, I flourished at Malvern; I passed my Grade 8 oboe exam with distinction and, early in my Upper Sixth year, I won the school's music prize, which boosted my confidence so much. I actually couldn't believe it, I had never won anything like that before, or been recognised in that way for anything.

My time at Malvern holds special memories. There was freedom, but also a certain childlike, whimsical, Enid Blyton-like innocence, which I loved. I volunteered to spend a term in The Annexe. Our housemistress must have been in her early sixties and she dressed like she had just walked out of a wholesome 1950s' book – below-the-knee wool skirts, neat-collared blouses, buttoned-up cardigans, grey hair neatly tied back in a bun. She had a twinkle in her eye and I liked her very much. Every weekend, we would receive a delivery of 'goodies' from the main kitchen – cheese, bread, cake, bacon, fresh eggs and we would cook snacks at all hours in our little kitchen.

While in the upper sixth I started a relationship with Adam, who was in the same year as me at Malvern College, the boys school. I adored him; I was madly in love – or so I believed at the time. We'd meet after school, and at weekends we'd sometimes go for fish and chips at a nearby hotel restaurant, feeling grown-up as we each savoured a glass of wine (the school rules stated that upper sixth pupils were allowed one alcoholic drink with a meal).

Adam and I spent as much time together as our respective timetables allowed. On weekdays, though, the girls had a 6.30 p.m. curfew. We had to sign a register when we returned to the boarding house, and our housemistress would be there in the office, waiting, ready to pounce on latecomers. After kissing Adam goodbye, I'd sprint back to the house – if you weren't home by 6.30 p.m. on the dot, you'd invariably be gated for a day or two. I got busted a few times. 'You're late, Liz,' my housemistress would say, tapping her watch and glowering at me through her half-moon glasses as she looked up from behind her writing desk. 'You're gated tomorrow.' My heart would sink whenever I heard that.

Being in a loving relationship, feeling wanted, meant so much to me. As an adoptee, I craved security and warmth from others and feared rejection – I still do today. I felt safe with Adam and sensed he was committed to our partnership for the long haul. He welcomed me into his family, and, our A-level grades permitting, we'd planned to go to the same university: Royal Holloway, University of London, in Surrey, where I'd been offered a conditional place to study a French and music degree.

I was thrilled that Adam wanted us to stay together through our university years. Back then, I'd daydream about him proposing to me one day. I visualised my wedding dress – a vintage-style, beaded affair like the gown Grace Kelly wore for her marriage in *High Society* – with a long veil fluttering down to my knees. I wanted the fairy tale.

Adam's family lived in Gloucester, so we often went to his house at weekends. His mum, Susan, fascinated me. She reminded me of Doris Day with her chin-length blonde hair, set in glossy waves, and her pretty outfits. Gentle and kind, she doted on Adam, which was lovely, but I admit, I found her affectionate gestures towards him difficult to watch. She hugged and kissed him a lot and called him 'darling'. This kind of behaviour seemed foreign to me; there was never as much spontaneous hugging in our adoptive home.

* * *

In summer 1992, I passed my A-level exams, achieving an A in music, a B in French and two Es for history and general studies. Mum thought the history examiner had made an error of some description. 'Right, we're getting that paper re-marked,' she told Dad. I don't recall that we ever did query my history grade, but my results meant I could go to Royal Holloway as planned, with Adam, who'd also achieved the grades for his conditional offer.

I was sad to leave Malvern. I'd achieved a lot – personally and educationally – during my two years at boarding school. I hadn't forgotten about the facts contained in my adoption papers though; I would often wonder, *Why did Yvonne abandon me?* Or, *Why did she want an abortion?* I'd just managed to mask my feelings via my schoolwork and my joy at having a boyfriend. Now eighteen, I thought about how I would go about finding Yvonne, but it would take me time and courage yet to pursue that search. *What if I do find her but she doesn't want to know me?* That thought terrified me – I couldn't face another rejection from my birth mother. So, I decided to leave the matter for the time being as I headed to Surrey, with Adam, for another new beginning.

5

The Fog

I couldn't have wished for a more enchanting setting than Royal Holloway, University of London. Modelled on the Château de Chambord in the Loire Valley, the Founder's Building at Englefield Green, Surrey, is a stunning, sprawling composition of Victorian red-brickwork, complete with spires and curves and curious circular windows set in soaring turrets. Constructed around two verdant quads – one containing a statue of Queen Victoria – the Founder's Building has a fairy-tale charm.

For the first year of my four-year degree, I had a room in one of the halls of residence, in the Founder's Building. My room was furnished with a single bed, a desk, a slim wardrobe and bookshelves. A Victorian cast-iron radiator, painted magnolia, crouched below a window that framed glorious blood-orange sunsets on clear evenings, providing a beautiful background to the tips of the turrets.

I knew from the outset that I'd chosen the right course, despite still not knowing what I wanted to do when I eventually left university. The music part of my degree was especially fascinating. Alongside the practical element – performing recitals and honing my oboe and piano skills – we studied all facets of music, analysing pieces from the medieval period to the twentieth century. We studied the history of music, and music as propaganda in politics.

I worked hard and received positive feedback from my tutors. Socially, though, I wasn't entirely sure where I belonged. I was still with Adam – all seemed well in our relationship as far as I could tell within the first few months at Royal Holloway – and I'd made some lovely friends, but I struggled to know which pocket of people I fitted into. I'd look at the other girls in my year and think, *You all know who you are.* I didn't feel this way.

There were so many different groups at university, a plethora of personalities, characters and identities. I liked being among the diversity of my fellow students, but it made me question my identity further for a while. I wasn't a big drinker – I liked the sensation of becoming giggly after just one Malibu and Coke (my drink of choice – sweet, not bitter), but I didn't like feeling fuzzy-headed and 'out of control' after a couple of drinks. At parties or late-night gatherings I'd prefer more intimate, deeper conversations. I didn't play sports at university, so I didn't feel I belonged in the crowd of rugby girls, although I did spend a lot of time with the rugby boys. I was constantly searching for 'my people', and the confidence, those elements of 'Liz' I'd gained at boarding school, somehow ebbed as I again battled to figure out who I was.

As I grappled with my identity issues, I endured another rejection that hit me like a freight train. Shortly before the summer term ended, Adam split up with me. He told me our relationship wasn't 'working out' or something along those lines. I was distraught; we'd been a couple for eighteen months and I'd assumed we'd stay together. He said he was sorry, but I didn't want to accept that Adam and I were over. I couldn't believe that he wanted to toss aside our history, our love. I was distraught. I'd lost the person who'd made me feel safe and wanted.

I did, in time, move on after Adam. I didn't like being single. I craved closeness and affection; I needed the security, to be 'looked after' – I realise this now. I never had one-night stands, though. I had to get to know someone, to feel a level of trust and connection between us before being intimate with someone. I felt this way about my next long-term boyfriend, who came into my life at the beginning of my second year at university.

He first caught my eye in the lunch hall as I tucked into a jacket potato while chatting with my friend Belinda. I was struck by his towering, broad-shouldered beauty and modest smile beneath the brim of his baseball cap. My heart skipped a beat when he and his two friends sat down at our table. He took off his cap to reveal a crop of attractively ruffled light-brown hair. I couldn't stop staring at him; he had such a protective presence. I felt myself blushing when he said, 'How're you doing?'

'I'm Liz,' I blurted, smirking like a schoolgirl and clumsily unscrewing the cap on my water bottle.

He laughed, a big laugh that suited his swimmer-like frame. 'Good to meet you, Liz. I'm Tom.'

Tom and I chatted over lunch. He was also in his second year, studying Zoology, he told me. I spoke excitedly, nervous and smitten at once. And when he finally got up to leave, saying, 'See you around, Liz,' I wanted to ask him to stay.

After our first encounter in the lunch hall, I did see Tom 'around' frequently. I'd bump into him at the student union bar, at parties, in the lunch hall again. It was obvious we were attracted to one another and, within a few weeks, we became an item. I loved Tom dearly. He was gentle and considerate; I felt 'looked after' by him.

A few months into our relationship, which was a secure, stable partnership, I became withdrawn. It was like a light had suddenly been switched off inside me. I stopped going out so much with friends. Thoughts of my past overwhelmed me. I wasn't sleeping properly, racked with the same angst that had haunted me at night as a child. *I should be so happy*, I'd think. From a stranger's perspective, my life must have looked pretty perfect: I had a boyfriend whom I adored; I was studying at an amazing university; I loved my course, and I'd be spending my third year studying in Paris, which was a wonderful opportunity to look forward to. And I was hugely appreciative of all of those things. What I didn't have – and what many others couldn't see was missing for me – was 'my people'.

Eventually, I booked an appointment with the student counselling service, hoping that a professional might help me to navigate and better understand my emotions.

My session with the counsellor, a woman in her late forties called Tracy, lasted for almost an hour. From what I recall, I told her I was adopted, and she asked me to describe my relationship with Mum and Dad. I talked at length about Mum, explaining how controlling she was. 'I don't feel connected to my adoptive mother,' I said. 'She won't listen to me. She – and Dad – don't ask me how I'm feeling. I feel lost … just, really down.'

Tracy listened to me, but, like other counsellors I'd speak to in the years to come, she didn't acknowledge the trauma associated with adoption. I realised much later that this is because society is conditioned to view adoption as a good thing. The child has been saved – chosen – is often the mindset. Many people don't consider the challenges that adoptees face: we are legally severed from our natural parents, they're no longer our next of kin; although the same blood runs through us, we have no automatic right to inherit from our biological parents' estates. We are completely cut off. Most importantly, as adoptees, we grow up devoid of genetic mirroring. We can't see ourselves in our adoptive families because we don't share their DNA and this is a form of grief for us, almost universally unrecognised by society. Only specialised counsellors, ones trained in this very specific form of trauma, can even begin to understand this pain. Nevertheless, some still don't get it.

My counselling meeting ended with Tracy saying, 'I think you have clinical depression, Liz.' She referred me to the university's GP, then I was assessed by a psychiatrist, who confirmed this condition and prescribed anti-depressant pills. My diagnosis shocked me; at the time I thought, *I'm not 'clinically depressed'. Traumatised, misunderstood, very sad deep inside, yes, but ... depressed, really?* Nonetheless, I went along with the diagnosis. I took the tablets and read self-help books about coping with clinical depression. Looking back, I now know I was in 'The Fog', a term describing the fear, obligation and guilt felt by many adoptees. Consciously or subconsciously, adoptees may employ these emotions to mask the trauma of being separated from their birth mothers. Being in The Fog – or coming out of The Fog – I'd later realise, is a hugely impactful process, almost as if we are being reborn, blessed with a realisation, an acknowledgement, a spiritual transformation even.

So I did what I was told, swallowing the tablets alongside the gut feeling I had that 'clinical depression' was *not* the root of the problem. The side effects were unpleasant, so the dosage needed tweaking. But the side effects persisted, so another type of antidepressant was prescribed. Despite every prescription, every new drug, my feelings and thoughts remained. Deep down, I knew something else was at play. I had no idea as I took those antidepressants just how severe my adoption trauma was;

I didn't understand it. A part of me thought the pain was normal because it had always been there, pain that I was prevented from suffering, forbidden to express.

On the weekend after my counselling session, Tom and I visited Mum and Dad in Harborne. Tom already knew about my 'clinical depression' and he'd been understanding, encouraging me to go to the counselling department. He hadn't judged me, and I valued his support. I might have known Mum and Dad wouldn't be as sympathetic.

To go home, with my boyfriend, and tell my parents, 'I've got clinical depression and I'm on tablets for it,' was a huge thing for me. That's why we made the trip – I wanted to tell them in person. To me, this was big, serious news, and I was hoping Mum and Dad would offer some comforting words, display perhaps a glimmer of recognition that I was going through a tough time. I'd taken one of my self-help books to show them, a title I was reading to try to understand my diagnosis.

'Why have you bought that book?' asked Dad, 'You're convincing yourself that there's something wrong with you.'

Mum fidgeted in her armchair, a spasm of distaste contorting her lips. 'Goodness, you're not depressed, Elizabeth. You don't have anything to be depressed about.' My heart sank at her comment. Her tone and face said it all: *Oh, my goodness, we can't have a daughter on anti-depressants. What will people think?*

My parents' dismissal of my 'depression' filled me with a horrible sense of shame. They'd completely shut me down at a time when I'd really needed their emotional support. All I'd wanted was to be heard, to be seen by them. They couldn't do that for me. Whether that was because they didn't understand or didn't *want* to understand almost didn't matter. I went back to university feeling as though I'd done something terribly wrong, like I'd let them down. The Fog, which I couldn't then fathom, continued silently to oppress me, engulf me, choke me.

Even in adulthood, my adoptive parents, Mum especially, shielded me from certain matters. They refused to have open conversations with me and tried to make decisions on my behalf. I felt such a disconnect from them; we weren't able to converse on the level of feelings. So I abandoned my efforts, realising the futility of my attempts to emotionally connect with them, deciding instead to trust in myself.

Illness and death were other taboo subjects in our home. When Andrew and I were growing up, Mum didn't cope well if we were unwell. On occasions when I fell ill at school, Mum would come to collect me, but I somehow felt like I was being an inconvenience. When I felt sick, I was left kneeling over the toilet bowl alone while she waited in the kitchen. No hair-holding or back-stroking. (Cue a serious fear of vomiting from childhood). Likewise, if I injured myself – cut open my knee after falling off my bike, for instance – Dad would deal with the gory bits and stick on the plaster. Mum later admitted to being 'squeamish', which I found strange. Tending to your children when they're poorly or injured, dealing with the blood or vomit or diarrhoea without complaint, awkwardness or hesitation should just be par for the course of being a mother.

Mum simply couldn't deal with medical issues. I remember her sheer panic whenever poor Nanny Mac suffered a 'funny turn'. Those episodes started when I was in my late teens. She'd suddenly fall silent and her eyes would glaze over as she lost consciousness. When she eventually came round, she'd be terribly sick. It broke my heart to see Nanny Mac in this state; my instinct was to help her, but Mum would shoot out of her chair, ushering me out of the room, her voice loaded with fear.

Medics later said Nanny Mac had probably suffered a series of mini-strokes, yet the term 'funny turn' seemed preferable to admitting what was really happening to her.

I was around twenty when my adoptive nan on Dad's side, moved into a hospice. This news shocked me. I discovered that Nan, a nurse in her younger years, had cancer somewhere, but all my parents told me about Nan's illness was, 'She was bleeding from places where she shouldn't be bleeding', the inference being that Nan had left it too late to seek medical help.

One Friday evening in winter 1993, I arrived home in Harborne for a break from university. Mum and Dad were expecting me, but they weren't home. Mum called the house phone about ten minutes after I'd let myself in to say she was at the hospice with Dad. 'I don't think Nanny will last very long now,' she said, and my immediate inkling was to go to the hospice to say goodbye to Nan. Although I'd never felt much warmth from Dad's mum, I was upset to hear she was about to die.

'I'm coming to the hospice,' I told Mum. 'I want to say—'

'Oh, no, no, no, no, no, I don't think that's a good idea. I think you should stay away, Elizabeth.' Mum said a hurried goodbye and that was the end of the conversation. I didn't go to the hospice. Mum had made it clear that she didn't want me there. Nan passed away later that evening. My parents didn't speak about Nan's final moments when they came home. I wondered what Nan's last words, if any, had been, and I hoped she'd died peacefully. Above all, I felt sad that I hadn't had the chance to say goodbye to her. Endings, closure – I struggled with them. I never processed them well, as a therapist would help me learn and explore almost thirty years later.

By the time I reached my third year at university, I felt happier within myself. In September 1994, I moved to Paris to study at The British Institute. Before I left, I ended things with Tom. This was the first time I'd broken off a relationship – and I felt awful doing so – but something was telling me that Tom wasn't 'the one' for me. And I wanted to make a fresh start in Paris.

I have such fond memories from that year. I shared an apartment with my university friend Belinda – or Bee as she was by then known – on Rue Championnet, just a twenty-minute walk north of Montmartre. Compared with my hectic study schedule in the UK, work was more relaxed in Paris. I had only eight hours of lectures a week, but I did have to operate entirely in French.

There was a small group of us from Royal Holloway studying in Paris, including my friends Laura and Pete, and we enjoyed making the most of the beautiful city, doing all things Parisian: sitting outside Art Nouveau cafés drinking strong coffees, smoking cigarettes and eating flaky, melt-in-your-mouth croissants; visiting galleries and tourist attractions such as the Eiffel Tower and The Louvre. We were so lucky to have this cultural paradise on our doorstep. Some evenings, we'd sit on the steps of the Sacré-Coeur, as the sun cloaked the busy city in calming shades of amber, rose and orange and sing along to Pete's guitar playing. Those were idyllic times when I finally experienced freedom, connection and belonging.

Being in a smaller friendship circle than at home, I found it easier to socialise. In photographs from that year, I look vibrant, much more comfortable in my own skin. There's a picture of me leaning out of the kitchen window of our apartment, overlooking the busy street below. I remember smiling at Bee, who was leaning out of the adjacent window, pointing her camera and shouting, 'Say cheese.' She captured me just as the sun was setting, bathing my smiling face in golden light.

I adore this picture; it has an otherworldly quality. And that's where I was – in another world. I was happy.

I thrived in Paris; being away from the UK, speaking another language was a wonderful distraction and helped me to mentally detach from my feelings. By the end of the year, I was fluent in French. I didn't want to come home, but I was grateful to have had the opportunity to study abroad. It really opened my eyes and mind ahead of my final year at university. But before I started that year, another loss came.

My beloved Nanny Mac passed away in a care home in the countryside just outside of Harborne. As she'd reached her early nineties, Nanny Mac could no longer manage living alone in West Bromwich, particularly when her memory faded, hence her move to the care home. She clearly had dementia, but Mum was hesitant to acknowledge this. 'She's happily confused,' she'd say light-heartedly about her mother's illness.

Dear Nanny Mac had lived to a good age, but this did not assuage my grief. She'd played a huge role in my childhood, and I'd felt privileged and proud to call her my grandmother. The way she'd treated me, with genuine affection, had felt almost maternal. A small part of me died with her.

On the day of Nanny Mac's funeral, before the hearse carrying her arrived at my parents' house, I stood alone on the front lawn, strewn with bouquets of flowers. I read the messages on the cards accompanying the sprays, crying quietly at the kind tributes that evoked memories of her.

At Mum's request, the funeral procession involved a tour of West Bromwich, stopping for a moment outside Nanny Mac's former home. From the back of the funeral car, I gazed at her old front door, at the leaded light windows veiled by net curtains, remembering the smell of dolly mixtures, her snowy hair and twinkly smile. I heard her gentle voice in my head: *How's my little piccaninny?* and I said a silent goodbye to her as we slowly pulled away from her house.

Losing Nanny Mac hit me hard, reigniting thoughts about finding Yvonne. I figured my first step towards searching for her would be to write to my adoption agency, but still I feared my mother might not want to know me. *Is she out there? What happens if I do find her?*

Towards the end of August 1995, I finally wrote a letter to The Children's Society, asking for records relating to my adoption. I didn't tell my parents about this letter; I was conscious of how they would feel about it. I validated this decision by telling myself, *I'm an adult now. I'm not living under their roof, and besides, this is* my *heritage,* my *story: I want to find* my *birth mother.*

Naturally, I was apprehensive, scared even. *What if my search ends here?* I did my research and discovered the National Adoption Contact Register, which matches adoptees with birth parents wishing to contact one another. I signed up to have my name put on the register. My only hope of meeting Yvonne rested on whether she had also added her name to this roll. Whether she wanted to be found was in the hands of fate.

I posted the letter, my stomach twisting and gurgling with nerves while bracing myself for a long wait for a response.

To my surprise, a senior practitioner from The Children's Society replied to my enquiry within days. I sat on my bed, trembling as I read the second line of the letter: *I am writing to confirm that The Children's Society does hold records relating to your adoption.*

In her response, the practitioner said the next step would be to arrange an appointment for me to speak with a post-adoption counsellor – to 'discuss if and how to contact natural relatives'.

She'd also enclosed a four-page A4 booklet containing a suggested reading list, information about the society's procedures, and a section titled 'Approaching Reunion'.

A few weeks later, I met Jenny, my assigned post-adoption counsellor, at The Children's Society's offices in Peckham, South London. Jenny immediately put me at ease. She had a motherly tenderness about her, from her lilting voice to her neat brown curls. She spoke slowly and deliberately, as I'm sure she had been trained to do.

'I know this must be difficult for you,' she said softly, 'something that you've obviously been considering for some time. But we do have your adoption records, and I can confirm that your birth mother has also joined up to the National Adoption Contact Register, like you did, and has signified that she'd welcome contact.'

'So she wants to know me? She's been looking for me?' My voice came out smaller and quieter than I had intended. This was a lot for me to take in.

Jenny smiled. 'Yes, Yvonne has expressed her wish to be contacted.' She talked about the reunion process and, as I'd read in the booklet posted to me, Jenny said this can often feel like an 'emotional rollercoaster': 'Reunions can bring up a lot of intense feelings from the past. Sometimes, the euphoria of having found one another is replaced by feelings of sadness and loss. Reunions can impact hugely on the adoptive parents, too – they might feel resentful or left out of the process. Sometimes they fear they'll lose the child that they brought up and loved.'

One factor of adoption reunion that had shocked and nauseated me when I'd read about it in a separate booklet Jenny handed to me was Genetic Sexual Attraction (GSA). GSA describes the physical feelings that can occur between estranged blood relatives when they're reunited later in life. As Jenny explained, 'This is rare, but in some cases, people's emotions become so heightened that they get sexually confused. This is seen as a natural result of the bonding process, which was cut off during infancy.'

I was too excited to deal with that troubling thought in the moment, so I tucked that leaflet beneath the pile of booklets on the desk before me. I asked Jenny, 'So what do I do now? How do I reconnect with Yvonne?' The conversation felt almost surreal.

'Well, should you and Yvonne wish to accept contact, I will act as an intermediary. I would suggest exchanging letters in the first instance. This will give you the opportunity to get to know your birth mother without direct contact.'

I agreed with Jenny. Letter-writing seemed like a nice, gentle approach. We spent the rest of the meeting discussing what I'd learned so far about my beginnings and I told Jenny about my fear of being rejected again by Yvonne.

Jenny put her head on one side. 'Don't feel you need to rush into a reunion. There are no rights or wrongs. It's about feeling comfortable with how things are progressing, and I'm here to offer support and guidance along the way. Just take things at *your* pace.'

I left The Children Society's office and walked to the train station in a daze. *Where do I start?* I had so many questions I wanted to ask Yvonne. On the one hand, it was comforting to know that she wanted to hear from me. On the other, I was cautious about the painful wounds a reunion might expose. *Am I ready for this?* Deep down, I knew I would pursue contact with Yvonne but, as Jenny had said, I could do this at my own pace. This wasn't something I should rush into.

After much consideration, and out of courtesy, I decided to tell my parents that I'd contacted The Children's Society. That was a discussion I'll never forget.

A few days after my meeting with Jenny, I called home from the landline in the student house I shared. That phone was in the silliest of places – it was a big grey thing, mounted on the wall at the bottom of the stairs, right in the thoroughfare – if you wanted privacy, forget it.

Dad answered the phone. I waited for the right moment to tell him, after we'd caught up, then said something like, 'I decided to find Yvonne. I had a meeting with The Children's Society, and Yvonne has also signed the National Adoption Register, like I did. She wants to have contact with me.'

Dad fell silent. I could hear the clocks doing their usual thing in the background. 'We're disappointed,' he said finally, 'disappointed that you didn't tell us and ask for our support with this.' The one word I remember from the conversation that day, ringing clear to me even now: 'disappointed'. In the depths of my memory, the words that ensued were just a blur. I still can't access them, as I'm tightly shutting my eyes, trying to focus on what else was said. He said goodbye, and then he was gone.

I replaced the receiver and sat on the bottom stair, motionless. Fortunately, my housemates were out. The house stood still and silent around me. I wanted to be hurt, angry at his reaction, his words, but all I felt was shame. I wanted my parents to be proud of me for plucking up the courage to find my birth mother, for being strong and brave. I wanted them to ask me so many questions, to *engage* with me: *How was that meeting with Jenny? Is she nice? Did she make you feel comfortable? Did you find it difficult? Did you get upset? Oh, that must have been so hard for you. I can't imagine how you must have felt.*

Such a big thing for you. They never would say such things. I felt I'd done the wrong thing in their eyes, like I'd gone about it in an inappropriate way. But finding Yvonne was never *for* them. It was never *about* them. I did it for *me* – ungrateful, unappreciative, uncaring and inconsiderate *me*.

I hadn't realistically expected Dad to be over the moon at my announcement, but his reaction left me feeling numb. However, I resolved, as I sat there on the stairs, that I would write to Yvonne. When the time felt right.

6

What about My Cuddle?

In the summer of 1996, I graduated from Royal Holloway with a 2.1 BA Hons degree in music and French. Although pleased with this result, I had no job lined up, so I returned to Harborne, telling myself, *This is just a stopgap until I figure out what I want to do.*

Going home to live with my parents was a step backwards for me. Despite its multitude of clocks, the house felt timeless, unchanged. The Royal Doulton ladies assumed their same positions on the coffee table, faces frozen in saccharine smiles. Jif fumes lingered in the Hall of Mirrors bathroom, and the antique furniture gleamed, its history almost wiped out by rigorous polishing. Everything looked untouched.

Mum sat in her armchair every evening, watching TV, tut-tutting at controversial soap storylines. Dad listened to his music when Mum went to bed. They went to church on Sundays and dinner was served punctually at 6 p.m. during the week. They hadn't changed, but I had.

Almost a year had passed since my meeting at The Children's Society, when my post-adoption counsellor Jenny had told me the news I'd been longing to hear since I was a child: my birth mother, Yvonne Watts, had been searching for me. I was yet to write my first letter to Yvonne. My last year at university had been too hectic and stressful to even consider composing my first words to my birth mother. Even now that I'd finished my degree, I didn't feel in the right place mentally to put pen to paper. I wanted to, but it wasn't a straightforward affair; finding the right words would take time, and an emotional capacity I hadn't quite reached yet. I couldn't just rattle off a letter saying, *Hey Yvonne, I hope you're well, so glad we're in touch now*, etc. I was conscious, as Jenny had pointed out, that the reunion process would heighten all kinds of emotions in me *and* Yvonne.

I thought about Yvonne every day, wondering what she looked like, how she spoke, what her hobbies were. *When did she start looking for me? She's forty-two now – did she have another child after me? More than one child perhaps?*

Being back under my parents' roof, in the house of pretence and unspoken truths, sparked some painful memories. Every time I looked at the tasselled footstool in the lounge, I saw myself, aged sixteen, sitting there with my adoption papers on my lap, reading that my birth mother had given me up for adoption after being refused an abortion. I did want to hear Yvonne's side of the story, but I was still in a place of hurt, still fearing she'd reject me again. *It was too soon to write.*

It goes without saying that Mum and Dad didn't talk about my efforts to find Yvonne. For all they knew, I might have met her already. As usual, this topic was ignored, but they would openly discuss my career options. Mum had some suggestions. It was the same conversation every day.

'You must do something with your degree, Elizabeth,' Mum would say. 'You should become an MP. Or you could be a translator. They're both well-paid jobs. Failing that, I suppose you could go into teaching.'

I didn't want to be an MP or a translator. Teaching might be a possibility at a push, I reasoned. Truthfully, more than anything, I was desperate to be a mum – a *good* mum. One day. In the meantime, I did need to find a job, preferably a job far away from Harborne.

'Well, I'd like to work with people. I'd like to help people,' I'd reply, and Mum would look at me as though I was an abstract work of art she couldn't comprehend.

I felt stifled again. I missed my uni friends. Andrew was away at university in Carlisle and yet to come home for the summer break. I spent most days working on my CV and scouring career supplements in newspapers, or hanging out with my friend Chris, much to Mum's disdain.

Chris was the same age as me and lived a few streets away from my parents. We'd take his dog for walks or go to the White Swan pub in Edgbaston. Sometimes I'd go to his place where we'd chat and listen to music, but we couldn't do that at my parents' house. 'No going up to your bedroom with that boy,' Mum warned me whenever I mentioned Chris was coming over.

I told her, 'I'm an adult. Why can't Chris be in my bedroom? He's my *friend*.'

'You *know* why, Elizabeth' was always Mum's curt response, said with a strict headmistress-y glower on her face.

'Right, we'll go out instead then.' Her no-boys-in-the-bedroom rule was ridiculous, infantilising. I felt so awkward whenever Chris came to the house, having to explain to him that we, as two adult platonic friends, couldn't sit together in my bedroom.

I had to leave home, get a job, fast. *But how?* I'd only been home a few weeks and already I felt like a teenager again, suffocated and misunderstood by my parents, enduring Mum's broken record remarks: *What are you going to do with your degree? Why are you wearing that awful, manly shirt? Don't put the milk carton on the breakfast table, Elizabeth – go and get a little jug. No going up to your bedroom with that boy.*

I couldn't breathe.

Then, ironically, my parents facilitated my escape from Harborne. One of their friends and part of The Gang, had a high-flying job in human resources at at a major accountancy firm, and the department was looking for a graduate recruitment assistant. The job would be based in the company's London office at Embankment. 'This sounds like the perfect job for you,' said Dad, 'human resources, working with people. You should apply for it.'

I needed no encouragement; granted, accountancy and maths didn't interest me in the slightest, but the 'human resources' environment sounded exciting – as did a move to London. *Anything to regain my freedom*, I thought. I immediately applied for the job.

Everything happened so fast. I attended an interview at the firm on a Monday afternoon, and the following Saturday, a letter landed on the doormat. One word jumped out at me when I opened the letter: 'successful'. The human resources job was mine should I choose to accept it, which, of course, I did. Two weeks later, I moved to London. Freedom again, at last.

* * *

Living in the big city was both daunting and exhilarating. It took me a while to adjust to the manic pace of London: crowds of commuters, elbowing their way to and from work, spilling like hyperactive beetles from the throats of Tube stations; busy shops and streets choked with traffic; sirens screaming, the occasional shuddering whir of a police helicopter overhead.

But I loved the transitional energy of London – ever-changing, constantly reinventing itself. I was enjoying doing the same myself.

Fortunately, a former schoolfriend, Pippa, had also recently moved to London, so we decided to share a flat together. We found a two-bedroom townhouse in Parsons Green, south-west of the city.

The firm's offices were housed at 1 Embankment Place, a huge, arched building resembling a spaceship, towering above Charing Cross Station.

I felt so proud and independent entering that building every morning, striding across the atrium floor, dressed in my typically late-nineties oatmeal-coloured Balmoral plaid trouser suit – I always wore a trouser suit to work as I didn't feel comfortable in skirts and heels – my briefcase-style handbag in one hand, *The Financial Times* in the other. I confess, I'd only skim-read that newspaper, a prop to help me look the part and fit into my new corporate surroundings.

Always early for work, I'd often stop to chat to Tony, the concierge, dapper in his suit, as others hurried past, desperate to get to their first meetings of the day.

My job was indeed people-oriented; I interacted with scores of graduates, many of whom were barely younger than me. I met them at the interview stage and during workshops that I helped to run, both at the London office and off-site at Latimer House in Buckinghamshire. I enjoyed engaging with the graduates, hearing their stories, and helping them shape their careers.

Work was always busy, and time seemed to pass more quickly than ever in London. Before I knew it, six months had gone in a flash. Around this time, early 1997, I moved back to Surrey, into a lovely red-brick terraced house that Mum and Dad had just bought in Englefield Close, Egham.

They thought it made sense to invest in a property to save my paying rent to a landlord. As a financial director, Dad was clever with his money, astute with his investments. 'I'd rather we make good use of the money we have now, while I'm still alive, than after I'm gone,' he'd always say. I was truly thankful for my parents' generosity. I'd missed Egham a lot; many of my friends were still at Royal Holloway, so I'd now get to see more of them. The only drawback was my three-hour daily commute to work and back, but this didn't bother me initially. I loved being back in my familiar – and calmer – surroundings.

One Saturday evening, soon after I'd moved into my new house, I met up with a group of Royal Holloway friends at The Happy Man pub, a favourite haunt from my university days.

It was so lovely be with everyone again, especially my good friend Dan Harvie, best known as Harvie, whom I hadn't seen in almost two years. Nowadays, I suppose we would have kept in touch via texting or social media, but this wasn't an option back then.

I first met Harvie in my final year at university, soon after I returned from Paris. He was in his second year then, studying music and drama, so he attended some of the same lectures as me.

I'd warmed to him from the get-go. We spent so much time together during my final year at university. I'd go to his house-share, or he'd come to mine, and we'd sit up into the small hours, talking, laughing and singing. I could listen to Harvie sing forever; he has a beautiful voice.

We just clicked. Some of our friends used to say, 'You and Harvs should get together, you two are made for each other.' They had a point. You could say he was my 'type': tall and protective-looking with his sporty physique. He played for Royal Holloway's first football team and also represented

London Universities and the South of England Universities combined teams. He also made me laugh, often until my stomach hurt. His bear hugs were the best, too. But Harvie and I were simply close friends, and I'd cherished our relationship, that closeness, during my time at Royal Holloway.

He looked just the same when I met him in The Happy Man. His hair was still golden-retriever blond, short at the sides, but a little longer and wavy above his forehead. I squealed when I saw him, breathed in the memorable scent of Calvin Klein's 'One' as he squeezed me into one of his hugs which felt like home.

It was great catching up with my friends, but I spent most of the night chatting with Harv. We laughed as we reminisced about our late-night escapades, heading out in my little red Vauxhall Nova with the music blaring to bomb down to the local 7-Eleven for midnight snacks.

I told him about my job and our new house. 'I've just moved back here, into number eight, Englefield Close, so we can hang out again now,' I said.

Harvie's eyes widened. 'No way! How long have you lived in Englefield Close? I've been living on St Jude's Road for a few months, in the house diagonally opposite yours.'

'That's ridiculous! You've been over there all this time.'

I remember thinking that evening, as warm laughter and conversations flowed around me, *I'm happy, happy in The Happy Man, with my friends, with Harvie.* I felt at home.

From then on, we picked up where we had left off. Despite my long commute and Harvie's work, we still managed to spend a lot of time together, and with our friends. He was a tonic; his friendship meant the world to me. He had a big presence, yet he was so comforting, with a calming aura about him.

I hadn't really spoken in depth to Harvie about my adoption back in my uni days. I'd had plenty of opportunities to during some of our late-night deep and meaningful conversations, but I didn't. I didn't want to broadcast or face up to my past, not really. But now, as our friendship grew even stronger by the day, I started to open up to him a little. I told him, as we sat watching TV at my house one evening, about the day I discovered that Yvonne had joined the National Adoption Register and how I was still trying to muster the strength to write my first letter to her. 'I'm scared,' I admitted. 'What if she's changed her mind? What if she doesn't write back?'

Harvie folded my hand in both of his, forming a soft, reassuring pocket of comfort. 'I'm here for you, Liz,' he said, 'Always. I think you'll know when the time is right to reach out to Yvonne.'

My eyes watered. 'Thanks, Harvs, that means everything to me.'

* * *

I remember well the day when the 'right time' came, when I finally felt courageous enough to write to my birth mother. That serendipitous moment happened just before Christmas 1997.

I was on my lunch break from work, looking at magazines in a shop at Charing Cross Station when Slade's 'Merry Xmas Everybody' crashed through the overhead speakers. I shivered at the opening bars. A nostalgic shiver as I remembered a card a friend had given to me on my last birthday, one of those cards that lists key events that happened on the day you were born. My list for 11 January 1974 had included this line: '"Merry Xmas Everybody" by Slade was number one in the UK pop charts.' I returned the magazine I'd been flipping through to its stand, thoughts of my birthday and Yvonne playing alongside Slade in my head. *What happened on that day, almost*

*twenty-four years ago? Did Yvonne cry to this jovial song –
perhaps it played on a radio in the hospital when the midwife
cut the umbilical cord? Did Yvonne hold me against her breast,
kiss my little head, still warm from her womb, and whisper,
'Claire'? Was she even allowed to hold me, feed me?* I'd been
masking such questions for so long, but now, as 'Merry Xmas
Everybody' reached its climax, I somehow knew I was ready to
hear Yvonne's story – *our* story.

Before going back to the office, I called Jenny at The
Children's Society. I'd spoken with her a few times since our
meeting and she'd been so supportive, reassuring me that I
could take the reunion process at my own pace.

'I think I'm ready to write to Yvonne,' I told her from the
payphone on the concourse of Charing Cross Station.

'Okay, Liz, let me talk you through the process.' Jenny said
she'd let Yvonne know that I'd initiated contact between us. 'If you
send your letter to me, I'll forward it to Yvonne, and vice versa.'

'Thank you. This is a huge step for me.' We ended our call,
and I went back to work, now facing a new dilemma: *What
would my first words to my mother be?*

I didn't rush into writing my first letter to Yvonne. This
was a monumental process for me and I needed time to
compose my thoughts, to find the right words. So, I waited for
my birthday to pass – the day of the year when my adoption
trauma hits me hardest – until the end of January, then I sat
down at home with my pen and A4 pad and wrote my first
words: 'Dear Yvonne, …

It was difficult. There was so much I wanted to ask Yvonne,
but I was mindful of not steaming in with a barrage of questions.
That might deter her from replying to me.

In my letter, I explained how difficult and strange it felt to
finally 'put pen to paper'. I wrote:

I have to say that it was certainly a shock to discover that you had made an enquiry about me. I am a curious person by nature, so have often wondered about you – what you must look like, and the story behind my beginnings, but I never expected that you would be thinking those things too. I think that, subconsciously, I had prepared myself to never know much about you, other than what was available in my parents' adoption papers.

I am sure that we are experiencing things from very different sides, and I can only imagine what it must have been like to be in your situation twenty-four years ago, and to have to live with the situation for so many years could be difficult for you.

Now that I've got the hard bit out of the way, I just wanted to tell you a few things about myself:

Next, I wrote about where I grew up, explaining that I had a brother who was also adopted, but I didn't go into too much detail about my parents. I did mention Nanny Mac's death and how I still missed her. I let Yvonne know that I'd left university in 1996 and was now working in London for a 'large firm'. I decided to end my letter there, and signed off with 'Kind regards, Liz'.

I felt so nervous posting that letter. *Had I said too much? Should I have said more? Will Yvonne reply?* That was my biggest fear: that I'd hear nothing back. But Yvonne *did* reply – swiftly.

Harvie was with me when her letter arrived. We sat on the sofa together, me holding the envelope, mesmerised by the handwriting. Simple, round and friendly. I recognised the style from her signature on my original birth certificate.

'Are you ready?' he said.

'I think so.' I was in shock. This was my mother's writing. She'd touched this envelope with her fingers, licked the seal with her tongue. My flesh and blood were with me, in this very room. In my hands. I opened the letter, gulping hard as I read the first page:

Dear Liz,

I do hope that this letter finds you well.

I'm so glad that this moment has arrived, as I never thought it would.

I was so pleased to hear from Jenny just before Christmas, it seemed too much to take in at first, but now it has become real.

Where does one begin? I've waited such a long time to get this far, and never in all of 24 years have I stopped thinking about you and wondered what sort of life you were living …

Tears pooled in my eyes. 'She's never stopped thinking about me,' I said, as Harvie put his arm around my shoulder. I turned the page:

I was sorry to hear about your grandmother. But time is a healer, so they say. I myself have had a lot of upset in the last three years. I thought I'd never be able to pick up the pieces again. With everything that had happened in my life, I felt so dead and empty inside. There wasn't really much left for me. Then I met Martin and my life seemed to change for the better. We have been together for three years now and I think the world of him. We both think along the same lines and have a lot in common.

There was a lot of unhappiness and bad memories where I was living before, but now we have a brand new house and a fresh start in life. Mind you, moving house four days before Xmas was no joke – we didn't know whether we were coming or going …

In those paragraphs it was clear to me that Yvonne had suffered some big traumas in her life. I felt a heavy sadness in my chest with those seven words: 'There wasn't really much left for me.' I was pleased to hear that she'd found Martin, whom she clearly adored. I also caught a sense of Yvonne's personality. She loved her cats:

> I have a shaded silver Persian and three of her babies from different litters. The last one is fourteen weeks old and a ball of fluff. Sophie, the mother, takes a lot of grooming and has to be groomed every day so that the coat doesn't matt. Not that she always wants to be messed about – it takes a good half an hour and sometimes she just won't keep still. But at times I don't know what I would've done without them, they were my life.
>
> I have just changed my hours at work to full time and, working Saturday mornings, it's difficult to fit all the housework in as well as grooming the cats. Martin is very good though. If he doesn't work Saturdays, he normally does it for me, so I don't have a lot to do when I get home …

On the next page, Yvonne wrote that she worked as a checkout operator at Morrisons supermarket in Northampton, where she still lived. She wasn't 'that struck' by Northampton though:

> I was born in Romford and spent most of my early life around Essex. What relatives I have left are there and I try to get down as often as possible.
>
> My father worked for Ford Motor Co., and they got moved from Aveley up to here. Mum and I were on our own for the first two months and we hated it …

Yvonne's letter was eight pages long. She asked whether I visited my parents in Birmingham often, and about my job, which I thought was very sweet of her. I sensed, in her final sentences, she respected that I wanted to take things slowly, too:

> Anyway, I could go on forever. There are still many things to tell you, but I will leave it here at the moment. I'm really looking forward to getting your letter and hearing a bit more about you.
>
> Take care of yourself,
>
> Yvonne.

I stared at her name, thinking, *This is my real mother. These are her words, to me, her daughter.* It felt surreal; she had given birth to me and I shared her DNA, yet we were strangers.

'Are you okay?' said Harvie, who'd sat silently until now.

I folded the letter and popped it back into its envelope. 'She's never stopped thinking about me.'

* * *

Two months cartwheeled by before I got around to writing my next letter. A lot had happened in that time. London had become overbearing, too noisy and frenetic for me; I'm a country mouse at heart. And the commute was tiring; some evenings I wouldn't get home until after 8 p.m. So, I was thrilled when I landed a new job as a marketing assistant for American consumer goods corporation, Procter & Gamble, based in their offices in Egham.

The job offer came just days after I had written my second letter to Yvonne, in which I expressed how I'd grown up knowing there was 'somebody out there who was my flesh and blood', although they 'didn't even know me'. I assured Yvonne, however, that I'd had a 'fortunate, happy childhood'. I wrote about my interests, describing myself as being 'very musical and creative' and asked her whether I'd inherited these abilities from her. I was curious to know.

This period, around mid-April 1998, was one of big transitions. On 19 April, Harvie and I officially 'got together' as a couple. Looking back, I suppose it was inevitable that our friendship would become romantic; we were spending every available spare moment together and enjoying one another's company.

Our relationship developed naturally, but he told me after we had kissed for the first time, 'I've always held a candle for you, Liz – ever since I first saw you.' Those were the sweetest words. I had no idea he'd felt this way about me. Our friends weren't surprised when they saw Harvie and me cuddling in The Happy Man pub on that Sunday afternoon of 19 April. They just rolled their eyes and said, 'Oh, I guess you're finally an item now. Took your bloody time, didn't you?'

My relationship with him felt so right, so strong. We'd laid the foundations for this well with our enduring friendship. By now, Harvie had finished his degree and was working as a roofer while he figured out what he wanted to do career-wise. I worried about him doing the roofing job; he'd already had one accident when he'd lost his footing while working on the pitched roof of a five-storey hotel in London. He slid down the roof and ended up in a crumpled heap in the rain gulley above a two-storey drop onto the air-conditioning unit below. The only reason he hadn't fallen further was because his foot had become wedged in the gulley – terrifying.

He moved in with me straight away after we got together. We didn't know it then, but we would have some beautiful times, also some challenging ones, in that little house.

The following month, I received another letter from Yvonne. Harvie wasn't with me when it arrived; he was at work, on top of a roof somewhere. I sat on my wicker chair by the window in the lounge and opened the envelope, feeling braver this time.

I thought maybe Yvonne would write more about Martin and her cats, and hopefully answer some of the questions I'd asked her in my last correspondence. But she'd poured her heart out in this letter, which in turn broke my heart. It was raw, honest writing, revealing some details of my beginnings.

First, I was surprised to learn that Yvonne had started searching for me six years previously:

> You say in your letter it was a shock to discover I had made enquiries about you. It was like banging my head against a brick wall. I made a lot of phone calls to different people and wasn't getting anywhere fast. I nearly gave up hope in the end, but I was determined not to let it go.

Tears streamed down my face as I read the next few pages. Here, in her own words, is what Yvonne wrote:

> Perhaps you can't tell me but what information did you get from me from your adoption papers? I don't even know if you are aware of all the facts from beginning to end. Although you were aware someone, somewhere, was your flesh and blood, but you thought they didn't know you. Actually, I did know you a little bit.
>
> After you were born, I didn't see you straight away. All I knew was that I had a daughter, which I wanted desperately.
>
> The first time I saw you was at three o'clock in the morning. A little bundle wrapped in a pink shawl was handed to me, and

I cried my eyes out, knowing that I could never have you to keep forever.

I was in hospital for ten days of which I spent every minute possible being with you, feeding you, bathing and changing you.

There were three other people in my room, and I could only think how lucky they were to soon be going home with their babies.

Those ten days were the happiest of my life, and I shall never, ever forget them. The day I left wasn't so happy.

The social worker was coming at ten o'clock to collect you. I'd fed you, bathed you, and was getting you dressed all ready to go. But the social worker came at 9.30 a.m., and I didn't even get the chance for a last cuddle properly. I told her this and she said, 'Well, after you have handed the baby back to me, I will let you have her back for a short while.' Well, I handed you to her and she said, 'Okay, that's fine. Nothing else to do or sign, so I'll be off.'

'What about my cuddle?' I said.

'This child is no longer anything to do with you.' And with that she walked out of the room.

She was so abrupt and that upset me even more. I thought I'd never see you again, but I was told who the foster parents were, and I rang them up and asked if I could see you. Which I did for quite some time, normally twice a week. She was a very nice lady and understood my situation. She used to let me feed and change you, and I was grateful to her. I knew the time would soon be coming for you to be adopted and I still didn't want to let you go.

I pleaded with my father to change his mind and let me keep you. Even Mum had words with him, but the answer was still <u>NO.</u>

Eventually the day arrived, and my last visit had ended. I kissed you goodbye and asked you to forgive me, but I knew in my heart somehow, someday, I'd find you again …

I had to stop reading at this point. I hadn't even met Yvonne yet. I didn't know what her voice sounded like. Yet I heard her; she was speaking to me in those lines. *She'd wanted to keep me. I'd spent my first ten days with her. She had even visited me in the foster home. Am I imagining this, that after all these years believing that my birth mother didn't want or love me, she actually wanted to keep me?*

My shoulders shook. I dropped my wet face into my hands, and said aloud, in a broken voice, 'What about my cuddle?'

7

Getting to Know My Mother

I hadn't expected Yvonne to divulge so much information, to be so open about her emotions, so soon, but I admired her bravery.

Reading those first five pages of Yvonne's second letter was shocking and upsetting. I felt for her, and for me as a baby, forced to be apart when, according to her, she'd wanted to keep me.

I was also confused. Yvonne's sentences raised questions – questions which prompted more questions; everything was whirling around in my head. Details of Yvonne's story contradicted those contained in my adoption papers.

Once I'd composed myself a little, I re-read Yvonne's account of my first eight weeks in this world, trying to imagine how she – and I, as a vulnerable newborn – must have felt when I was taken away by the social worker. The wicker chair creaked as I sobbed. I felt that my body surely remembered, somewhere, the panic and terror of that moment; I heard my ten-day-old infant cries, sensed myself tightly parcelled inside that pink shawl. I imagined the abject, empty sadness Yvonne must have felt when she'd pleaded, 'What about my cuddle?'

Yvonne's inference was that her father had forced her to put me up for adoption: 'I pleaded with my father to change his mind and let me keep you. Even Mum had words with him, but the answer was still <u>NO</u>.' She said she'd desperately wanted a baby girl – was Yvonne denied that opportunity simply because she was young and unmarried? Had her parents seen me, held me? And what about my 'putative' father, Andrew Conant? *Was* he my father? Yvonne hadn't mentioned wanting an abortion, as stated in my original documents. Was that part of the report from 1974 a *lie*? It was too soon for me to broach this subject with Yvonne.

I continued reading her letter, in which she swiftly moved on to lighter affairs:

Your question about being musical and creative. It probably does come from me. I used to play the piano and organ, so did my father. My mother also played the violin and the organ.

I too am very creative. I love cross-stitch and stencilling and flower arranging, as well as many other things. I'm always making cakes of all types, and last Christmas I made my own cake and decorated it. Do you do much cooking? Are you living alone or with friends? I know you are a very cautious person, but you haven't really told me much about yourself or what sorts of things you like to do.

We've been very busy decorating our bedroom at the moment, and we still have the other two bedrooms, bathroom and en suite to do yet. There don't seem to be enough hours at the weekend to do everything. But, as the saying goes, Rome wasn't built in a day.

Martin is also trying to extend the patio. There is always something that needs to be done. How nice it would be just to get up and not have anything to do. Not much chance of that at the moment, though.

Well, I had better get the tea on as it's nearly time for Martin to come home.

Take care of yourself and I look forward to your next letter.
Kind regards,
Yvonne

I smiled at Yvonne's letter, at the palpable connection between my
blood mother and me. *I've inherited my musical and arty talents
from her. Inherited – the word had sounded foreign to me until
now.* I imagined Yvonne's house, furniture draped with old sheets,
the fresh smell of emulsion paint, her pottering around 'getting the
tea on'. I tried to picture her face, her mannerisms as she sighed,
'Rome wasn't built in a day.' Gradually, my mother was coming to
life on the page, but I still didn't know what she looked like.

I wrote back to Yvonne. I said I was sorry to hear she'd
suffered upset in her life, but I didn't ask her to elaborate. I also
expressed how difficult it must've been for her to 'give me up
for adoption when you really wanted to keep me'.

I wrote:

> You say in your last letter that you hope I can forgive you for
> what you did. I'm not at all surprised that you say you almost
> feel 'guilty' (if that's the right word) about it, but I have had
> a very happy childhood, and have had the opportunity to
> experience many things in my life. I actually think it was a very
> brave thing for you to have given me up for adoption.

Then, as Yvonne had requested, I told her more about my life. I
mentioned Harvie, talked about my job and shared with her my
love of 'cooking for people' and 'making things'. I said I would
send her a photograph of myself, and asked whether she'd like
to send me one of her.

About two weeks after I posted my letter, Harvie and I visited
my parents. I told them that Yvonne and I were exchanging

letters. Mum bristled, contorting her features into a puzzled frown. 'What's her name again?' she said, scrunching her eyes and wriggling her fingers about, as if trying to physically pull it in from the air. (This was not the first time my adoptive mother pretended that she couldn't remember my birth mother's name. It was one of the things about her that infuriated me throughout my life. It was disrespectful, both to me and to Yvonne, and it showed a disdain which turned my stomach.)

'Yvonne,' I replied firmly.

Dad surprised me, though. When I mentioned my intention of sending a picture to Yvonne, he said, 'I could take some photographs of you, if you like.' I appreciated his thoughtful gesture. He photographed me in their garden, and we got the film developed that same day. I was pleased with the pictures. I looked casual in my light-grey polo shirt, my blonde, shoulder-length hair brushing my shoulders in the breeze, as I smiled at the camera.

I sent a few photographs to Yvonne, accompanied by a few lines saying that I hoped we could meet one day but, for now, our letter writing seemed the best form of communication. As usual, Yvonne replied promptly. She hadn't sent me a photograph yet, but she said Martin was taking some of her and she'd forward them in her next letter. Her response to my pictures was heart-warming, and suggested a strong resemblance between us. My eyes welled with tears again.

You are a very pretty young lady and I'm proud to show your pictures to my friends and say that you're my daughter.

I must admit you were nothing how I imagined you to be, as when you were born your hair was auburn-ish in colour. Your hair colouring at the moment is almost the same as mine.

It's funny. I was really eager to see what you looked like, but I read your letter first, then took the photos out. I was by myself, and I cried when I looked at them. After all these years, at last I have something material.

Margaret, my next-door neighbour knew that I was waiting for the photos, so I took them in to show her. Her husband didn't know any of this, and when she showed him the pictures, he looked at them, then me, and said, 'Is this you when you were younger?'

I shall have to find some photos of when I was your age – they're somewhere in the loft, I think – but I can see the likeness, and so can Martin.

I only wish that my father was still alive because I'd show him your pictures and say, 'This is your granddaughter who you made me give up.'

Yvonne filled six pages of A4 paper, and once more, she disclosed personal, emotive information that answered some of the questions in my mind:

I really feel sometimes that I have missed out a lot in life not being able to have any children to bring up and have the joys of taking them to school – and then the growing-up stage.

I did fall pregnant nine years ago. I couldn't believe it when the result came through as positive, but when I went for my first scan, I knew something was wrong, but they wouldn't tell me.

The next thing I knew was that I was being rushed down to theatre as I had an ectopic pregnancy, and it was about to rupture.

I kept thinking to myself, why me? What have I done to deserve this – it's just not fair for this to be happening. That was a very traumatic experience to find out that, one minute, you're pregnant, the next, you're not. I felt so empty inside.

After some time, I decided to go for infertility treatment, which meant having two injections a day for ten days. Then a break, then start again.

I couldn't cope with going back and forth to the hospital every day. It was becoming difficult with work as they had to be given at the same time. I constantly felt like a dartboard, but I was prepared to try anything to become pregnant again, whatever it took.

After about a year, still nothing had happened, so I was put on a stronger injection which was more painful. It was uncomfortable at times, but I was determined to stick it out. Time was going on and it wasn't happening, then, one month, I really produced a good batch of eggs, and even the doctor thought that this was it. But it didn't work, and time was running out. I had one last chance to make or break. I was told that I only had one more thing to try, which was tablets and injections three times a day. We decided to go for it as I'd gone through this much pain – it couldn't get any worse. But it didn't work. They couldn't do any more for me, so it was stopped.

There were three other people going through the same as me, and it worked for two of them. Lucky people.

Poor Yvonne. Her experience must have been devastating – I couldn't begin to imagine the anguish of being told 'you can't have a baby' after so many attempts. After losing another child, again to an ectopic pregnancy. Yvonne didn't say who her partner was at the time, but it couldn't have been Martin. As she'd said in her previous letter, Martin had come into her life three years ago.

I enjoyed reading about Yvonne's home life, which she returned to on the next page in the manner of the calm after a storm. I found these passages comforting and amusing, hearing about her house renovations, Martin, the cats, and her cooking:

You said in one of your letters that you like cooking for people. So do I. We have our neighbours in a lot, and I cook a lot of stir-fries and Chinese food.

I have to make a fruit cake for Martin every now and again, but it doesn't last long where he's concerned.

A couple of weeks ago, I attempted a Black Forest gateau. It took a while to do, but I was quite pleased how it turned out.

Watching videos with a bottle of wine and a curry is something we do quite a lot on Saturdays. Some Saturdays we go into town, have a few drinks, and then go for a curry. Do you like curries? I couldn't stand the smell of them once upon a time, then a friend of mine said to try some of her meal. That's it now – I can't leave them alone.

Our lounge and dining room are decorated now, thank God, and everything is back in its place. For three days it looked like a bomb had hit it. I'm afraid I can't stand a mess, and I kept trying to make the place look tidy, but it was impossible. I gave up in the end.

Last weekend, we extended the patio, and the weather was kind to us – it didn't rain as forecasted.

I'm always pottering about in the garden, doing things, especially when the sun is out. Martin and I made a greenhouse up from a flat pack. That was a laugh, I must admit – there were that many nuts and bolts and screws, but we got there. Then we did a fishpond.

I also have two rabbits, and two of my cats have just had kittens, and I had to play midwife. They are seven weeks old now, so I shall be losing them soon. I hate parting with them,

113

and it's very hard not to get attached to them. It's like sitting at Silverstone circuit at the moment as they're having a mad half hour. They will soon collapse in a heap and go to sleep.

Already, I could sense myself in Yvonne. We shared the same interests – I too loved baking and pottering about in the garden. I'd told her in my last letter how I'd attempted to make salmon fishcakes: 'They went a bit wrong. They tasted alright but were about three times the size they should have been, and the breadcrumbs only covered about half of the fishcake, so I still need a bit more practice on that recipe.'

Yvonne's tone changed again at the bottom of page five, where she wrote about her recent meeting with Jenny, who, as agreed by me, had shown her my adoption documents. I breathed deeply, steeling myself for what was, or wasn't, to come on the next page. Yvonne must've seen the section referring to her wanting to abort me. I turned the letter over:

She [Jenny] showed me the records and what the social worker had written about me at the time. A couple of the things were untrue. Especially the part that said I had wanted to have an abortion and I hadn't told my parents.

I certainly didn't want an abortion. That was what my dad wanted me to do, and they [Yvonne's parents] were told about me being pregnant.

The social worker wasn't a very nice person, as I told Jenny, and even she [Jenny] said that sometimes they do write things down that are not quite correct.

Compared to that woman, Jenny was so different, very understanding. She knew how difficult it must have been for me to have gone through what I did.

So, Yvonne hadn't wanted to abort me after all. I believed her. The fact she'd visited me in the foster home proved she'd wanted to keep me. The message I took was that Yvonne had been subjected to a form of coercive control by her father. He hadn't approved of her pregnancy. Had he marched Yvonne, then only nineteen, into the doctor's surgery and said, 'She wants an abortion.' *Was that how the abortion line ended up in my file?* There was so much more I wanted to ask Yvonne, but we were still getting to know each other, tiptoeing along this reunion path. (Such a silly word for this, I thought – 'reunion'.) How can you be reunited with someone you have never met or known in your cognisant memory?

Harvie was with me when the chunky A5 envelope, decorated with Yvonne's neat handwriting, landed with a soft thud of announcement on the hallway carpet. Judging by the thickness of the envelope, I guessed it probably contained the photographs Yvonne had promised to send. Harvie was about to head off to work, but said he'd wait with me while I opened Yvonne's letter.

We sat down on the sofa and I fumbled with the brown package, quivering with nerves. I couldn't co-ordinate my fingers to open it. 'Here. Let me do that for you,' said Harvie.

I handed the envelope to him, watching as he carefully opened it. 'I'm so nervous,' I said, 'I've waited my whole life for this moment.' He paused, and put his hands on mine, fully present with me.

'Do you want to look now?'

'Yes,' I said, though when I regained possession of that envelope, I couldn't physically slide out its contents. I was worried the photographs would come out picture-side up and take me by surprise. I wanted to compose myself before seeing my birth mother's face for the first time. I passed the envelope back to Harvie to perform this impossible task for me.

'Right,' he said, 'are you prepared?'

I nodded yes and Harvie handed me the photographs. Immediately, I burst into tears. I saw myself in her. There she was, my birth mother, in a vivid clementine silky blouse, sitting in a floral armchair, her legs crossed and encased in sheer black tights. But her face! Her gaze met mine and she came to life. I forgot I was looking at a photograph; she was there with me, linked by flesh, and blood, yet still a stranger. Admittedly, I didn't see Grace Kelly in the picture, but I did see a forty-four-year-old version of me. I had her nose – level, but slightly tilted with longish, symmetrical nostrils. Her smile – straight, with a slight upwards tilt at its corners, was identical to mine. She had dyed blonde shoulder-length hair, softly permed, with a late-eighties-style flicked fringe. Gold hoops glistened in her earlobes. 'This is her, Harv. This is my *mother*,' I said, still staring at her, noticing her hand, resting daintily on her knee. Like me, she also has small hands.

'You really look like her,' Harvie said over my shoulder.

'I know,' I whispered, wiping my eyes, 'I know.' My tears were of relief, of confirmation, and sorrow at the lost years we'd missed out on.

Yvonne had sent a few photographs, including a couple of full-length shots of herself. The way she stood, her small frame, how she tilted her head to one side when she smiled was me all over.

I could've stayed there with Harvie for hours looking at those pictures and reading the letter that accompanied them. We both had to go to work, so I pulled myself together, but the image of my birth mother stayed with me all day, a powerful imprint, a reflection of myself branded onto my mind. I knew this image would never leave me again, that after all this time, I would finally be able to picture *her*, rather than trying to conjure somebody up from my own reflection in the bathroom mirror.

* * *

As Yvonne and I got to know more about each other via our letters, we also started speaking on the phone, which added a whole new dimension to our relationship, and brought her further to life. I could feel her becoming more tangible, more *real*.

Our phone calls started in summer 1998. Hearing Yvonne's voice for the first time was magical, it animated her from a flat photograph into a three-dimensional *person*. She had a very down-to-earth tone, with a slight Essex accent.

I'd look forward to chatting with Yvonne. We had similar personality traits, too; we are both ditsy, giggly, and very accident-prone. A typical phone call would start with Yvonne telling me she'd fallen down the stairs or had walked into a cupboard door. 'Oh Liz, you'll never guess what I did this week,' she'd say, and I'd usually have a similar anecdote about tripping over, walking into things or burning myself on a hot oven tray. There was so much laughter between us. Proper, heartfelt natural laughter – something I didn't often hear growing up.

I made Yvonne giggle with funny stories and sayings – and this felt so good. Sometimes, we'd laugh for minutes on end, prompting comments from Martin in the background. 'What are you two giggling about now?' he'd tease.

We'd ask each other questions, ones which, to an outsider, would have seemed mundane, like, 'What do you put in your cup first, the tea or the milk?' or, 'What's your favourite food?' We discovered that we both slept in the foetal position, on our left side, with our knees up to our chest. Our conversations were quite childlike at first as we tried to find shared moments and 'likes'. I felt I was coming home.

Naturally, I was still curious about my beginnings, and, thankfully, Yvonne spoke openly about this, even though it was upsetting for both of us. Gradually, throughout those conversations, the jigsaw pieces of my past slotted together. Yvonne took me back to when she discovered she was pregnant, relived the ten days she spent in hospital, recalled visiting me in the foster home and the harrowing moment she kissed me goodbye.

This is our story.

Yvonne was eighteen when she moved from Essex to Northampton with her parents, Leslie and Alfreda Watts. Soon afterwards, she started a relationship with Andrew Conant – known as Andy – who lived in her street. At that time, Yvonne was working as an admin assistant at the Express Lift Company in Northampton.

Around May 1973, Yvonne realised she'd missed a period or two. She panicked, thinking, 'Could I be pregnant?' She was nineteen and unmarried; in those days, pregnancies out of wedlock were considered unacceptable by society.

The exact moment that Yvonne discovered she *was* pregnant is unclear, but she knew Andy was the father because he was the only man she'd ever slept with. 'I must have gone to the doctor,' she told me. 'Because I don't think you could buy pregnancy tests over the counter back then.'

Eventually, Yvonne confided in her mother. She broke down in tears as she said, 'I'm late. I think I'm pregnant, Mum.'

Alfreda's hands flew to her temples. 'Oh my God, Yvonne, your father will go berserk.'

Leslie was a strict father. 'He was so pig-headed,' Yvonne said. 'Growing up, he'd slap the back of my legs if I'd done anything remotely naughty – that would really hurt.

'He was verbally abusive towards Mum, too. She used to suffer bad headaches that made her violently sick. Sometimes she'd pass out. I would tend to Mum, while Dad lay in bed or whatever. He wouldn't even help his wife when she was ill. "Oh, she'll get over it," he'd say. I *hated* my father.'

Yvonne and her mum were too scared to tell Leslie about the pregnancy, but as the weeks went by, they knew they had no option other than to break the news to him. By this point, Yvonne and Andy were no longer together. He was with a new partner, but he knew about the pregnancy and was supportive nonetheless.

As Alfreda predicted, Leslie went 'berserk' when she and Yvonne, both in floods of tears, explained the 'situation' to him. 'You're not keeping it,' he yelled. 'We're getting rid of it – and no one must know about this. You're a disgrace, Yvonne. How dare you bring trouble to our doorstep.'

According to Yvonne, Leslie had, as I'd suspected, frog-marched her into the GP's surgery and demanded a termination. She said, 'I can't remember how far gone I was, but I do remember sitting in the doctor's surgery with Mum and Dad. He said, "She's pregnant and she's having an abortion."

'The doctor examined me, then turned to Dad. "I'm sorry," he said, "but an abortion's not going to happen – it's too late for that."

'Dad got quite cross. "I still want it to go ahead. She's having an abortion and that's final."

'"Well." The doctor frowned. "So, you're willing to risk your grandchild's life as well as your daughter's? I'm telling you now, it's too dangerous." Dad got the hump at that and stormed out of the surgery.

'When we got home, he gave me the foulest look and said, "Well, if you're not having an abortion, you'll need to have it adopted." He was so abrupt; I didn't dare answer him back. I was frightened of Dad. I went up to my bedroom and cried and cried – I wanted to keep my baby. I thought, *Why can't I keep my baby? I'm not married, but why should that be an issue? We had three bedrooms, so there was enough space.*'

Yvonne had to hide her pregnancy. She wasn't allowed to see Andy either. Her father and Andy's mum, Val, colluded to keep their children apart as Yvonne became increasingly attached to me, growing inside her. She constantly begged her mother, 'Please can you speak to Dad, convince him to change his mind?' Alfreda did try, but Leslie's response was always a resounding, 'No, she's not keeping it. End of.'

As Yvonne's bump swelled – although she said she didn't begin to 'show' until around seven months – she shut herself in her bedroom in the evenings, knitting and crocheting baby clothes. She made little cardigans, bonnets and booties. 'I knitted everything in white or lemon, because I didn't know whether I was having a girl or a boy,' she recalled. 'I desperately wanted a baby girl, but the thought of that happening hurt me even more, knowing that I'd have to give her up.' Yvonne hid the baby clothes in her wardrobe. 'If Dad had found them, he'd have hit the roof.'

By December 1973, I was performing nightly can-can routines in my mother's womb. Yvonne laughed when she told me this – a laugh laced with sadness and regret. 'You were a small, wriggly bump, but you didn't half kick.'

Tears filled my eyes when she remembered visiting a Mothercare store with Alfreda: 'I wanted to put my baby in clothes that I'd chosen. I'd knitted loads of stuff already, but I needed some Babygros, so Mum and I secretly went shopping, behind Dad's back. As we rifled through the racks of tiny sleepsuits, I noticed a tear trickling down Mum's face. She brushed the tear away, thinking I hadn't seen it.

'If it weren't for Dad, I know Mum would have let me keep you, Liz – and she would've spoilt you rotten. Before I came along, Mum suffered a miscarriage, so she knew how painful it is to lose a baby.'

On the evening of 10 January 1974, Yvonne went into labour. She was in the lounge with her parents, watching *Coronation Street*, when the doorbell rang. The noise made her jump, which triggered her labour pains: 'It was Andy's mum Val at the door. She'd no doubt come round for a nose, to ensure I was at home and not parading my bump to the world. Well, she had to go away when I said, "My baby's coming." Mum helped me out to the car and Dad drove us to the hospital – and that was dramatic, I'm telling you. We got pulled over by the police. "You're speeding," said the officer. When Dad explained we were on our way to the Barratt Maternity Home, because I was in labour, the officer went, "Okay, follow me." The police escorted us to the hospital, blue lights flashing, sirens screaming.'

In Yvonne's words, as spoken to me, here's what happened from that evening onwards:

When we arrived at the hospital my contractions were coming fast. I'd never known pain like it. I felt frightened, not knowing what to expect.

I hobbled into the hospital building, holding Mum's arm, and the next thing I knew, a nurse was helping me into a wheelchair. I looked at Mum as I sat down. 'You will be with me, won't you?' I said as another wave wrenched in my midriff. 'I want you with me. I'm scared.'

Dad grabbed Mum's arm, pulled one of his stern looks. 'No, you're not going in there.' Then the nurse started wheeling me along the corridor. A few seconds or so later, I looked over my shoulder, expecting Mum to be behind me. She wasn't. She'd vanished. I thought, I can't believe I've got to go through this alone.

I got taken into a room. 'Where's my mum?' I asked as the nurse helped me out of my dress and into a massive tent-like gown. And I think the nurse said that nobody was allowed in the room with me for the birth.

My contractions continued throughout the night, into the early hours, when the time came for me to start 'pushing'. I screamed in agony, but I wasn't given any pain relief. The midwife told me to keep pushing while the nurse also stood at my bedside. 'You can squeeze my hand if you like,' she said, so I did – I left my nail imprints on her hand with my final push. And then it was over.

I heard you cry. 'Congratulations, you have a beautiful baby girl,' said the midwife, and I burst into tears. She looked confused then. 'I don't know why you're crying,' she said.

'Well, you obviously haven't seen my notes,' I said. I didn't get to hold my baby. The midwife disappeared out of the room with you. When she returned, without you, her mood had drastically shifted to one of sheer derision. 'I see the baby's flagged for adoption,' she said as another nurse wheeled a trolley equipped with stirrups into the room. 'Oh, and you need stitches.' With that, I was bundled onto the trolley. The nurse who'd let me squeeze her hand shoved my feet in the stirrups, glaring at me as she did so as though to say, 'You're a naughty, tainted, shameful girl.'

They pushed me out into the ice-cold corridor, where I remained, alone, terrified and shivering for over an hour. Again, I received no pain relief when the doctor finally stitched me.

I didn't get to see or hold you until much later that morning, and even then, I was only allowed two hours with you. I fed you, named you 'Claire Elaine', and I cried my eyes out. I was heartbroken – I wanted to keep you so much.

The same routine continued for the next nine days. They'd bring you to me in the morning so I could feed and bath you, then they took you to the nursery along the corridor, where you'd stay until the following day. I could look through the window into that room, but I wasn't allowed to go in there. About five rows of babies in plastic cots, spaced with military precision, filled the nursery. They always put you in the middle of the third row. I'd stand for ages at that window, looking at you, thinking, *Why can't I keep my Claire?*

I breast-fed you at first, then, after a few days, the staff put a stop to that. 'We need to get your milk to dry up now,' said one nurse. 'We'll give you something for that.'

It didn't help that I was in a room with three other new mothers, who had their babies with them all the time. I'd watch with deep envy when their husbands and relatives visited, armed with flowers and balloons, cooing over their newborns. I had none of this. Andy was escorted out of the hospital when he tried to visit me. 'You're not allowed,' he was told. Can you believe it? You were his daughter too – and he should never have been denied the chance to see you.

Mum and Dad visited me in hospital, but only once, and they weren't allowed to hold you.

Instead, we had to watch through the nursery window as a nurse held you up behind the glass. Dad bawled his eyes out when he saw you, which infuriated me. I stood up to him this time, though, knowing he couldn't go berserk in a public place. 'Why are you crying?' I said. Mum cuddled me – we were in floods of tears too. 'If it wasn't for you, it wouldn't be like this. This is your doing.' Dad wiped his eyes, glowered down at me, shrugged his shoulders then turned and walked away.

On our last morning in hospital, the social worker came into the ward, huffing and puffing. Reluctantly, I handed you to her and finished packing the clothes I'd bought and made for you into a bag. As I said, she'd promised to let me hold you one last time. She didn't. She put you into a carry-cot, grabbed the bag, and made for the door. That's when I asked her, 'What about my cuddle?'

The social worker left the ward, the hospital, with you. I didn't get my cuddle, didn't get to say goodbye to my Claire. I sobbed continuously. I felt as though my heart had been ripped out of my chest.

For the life of me, I can't remember who gave me the address and phone number for the foster home, but somebody kindly did leak that information to me.

Mrs Roberts, your foster mother, was very sweet and accommodating. Every morning, after Dad had gone to work, I'd drive to Mrs Roberts's house. I was only supposed to be there for an hour, but she always let me stay longer – sometimes I'd be with you for at least two hours. Mrs Roberts would make me a cup of tea, then leave me alone with you in the living room. I said to her, 'Don't feel you have to leave – stay and have a cuppa and a chat,' which she occasionally did. I told her about Dad and how he'd forced me to give you up. Mrs Roberts was ever so sympathetic – I think that's why she didn't mind my visiting. She understood my pain.

You were a contented baby. I'd bath and dress you, putting you in the new clothes I'd secretly knitted at home, then I'd give you your feed and settle back on the sofa, cradling you. Sometimes I'd read Beatrix Potter's *The Tale of Peter Rabbit* to you, and you'd gurgle away. I'd kiss your auburn hair and whisper, 'I'm so sorry, Claire. Please forgive me. I'll always love you, with all my heart.'

Behind the scenes during those six weeks, three couples were put forward to adopt you, but they were all unsuitable, apparently. I felt hopeful. I said to Mum, who knew about my visits with you, 'If this doesn't work out, will you help me try to get Claire back?' And she told me she would. Sadly, I was then told that a suitable family had been found. Oh, Liz, I was distraught. I thought about kidnapping you, but where would we go? I didn't have much money as I'd left work towards the end of my pregnancy, and I was yet to find a new job. I couldn't bear to give you up. We'd become so attached to each other.

I'll never forget the day the social worker took you from my arms. I'd already lost you once at the hospital, but this time, you were going for good. I was bereft – and deeply jealous of the lucky couple who'd soon become your parents. I thought, It's not fair. Those strangers will enjoy all the precious moments that I, as your mother, should experience: your first tooth, first steps, first day at school, birthdays and Christmases.

You left in a pink cardi and bonnet that I'd made for you. I kissed you, breathed in your scent – you smelt of Johnson's Baby Powder and sweet milk – and said for the last time, 'Please forgive me.'

Mrs Roberts's front door closed with a soft click. Next, I heard a car engine rumble to life outside. The sound faded, and then you were gone.

Afterwards, I sat in my car for at least an hour, crying uncontrollably, utterly heartbroken. 'They've taken my baby,' I sobbed.

I wanted to go to the adoption hearing at Birmingham County Court. Mum was going to come with me. In the end, a woman from the Church of England Children's Society advised me not to go. 'It'll be too traumatic for you,' she said. So, I didn't go, and I had to continue with my life not knowing where you'd gone or who was looking after you. I felt empty, lost. I didn't eat or sleep very well, didn't want to go out or speak to people. I never, ever forgave my father, and I thought about you every day. Wishing, praying that one day you'd find me.

* * *

Yvonne and I would go over her account numerous times. We still do today. She was treated barbarically in the hospital. Not allowing Yvonne to hold me following the birth was bad enough, but it surprised me that she was then allowed to spend ten days with me. Yvonne bonded with me in that time – despite me being sent to the nursery, along with the other babies flagged for adoption – then the mother-baby connection was brutally severed. Newborn puppies aren't allowed to be taken from their mother until they're at least eight weeks old, yet the authorities deemed it perfectly acceptable to separate Yvonne and me so soon after my birth. That was cruel and traumatic for both of us.

While I welcomed my newfound connection with Yvonne, I still approached our relationship cautiously. We continued to write to each other and chat on the phone, but even after several months, I still wasn't ready to meet her in person. Yvonne was sympathetic about this. 'We'll go at your pace, Liz,' she said. 'If you want me to back off at any point, just say.'

Sometimes, I couldn't get my head around my situation. I just couldn't call Yvonne 'Mum'. That didn't feel right somehow; I already had a 'mum'. Yes, our relationship was challenging, but she'd brought me up, fed and clothed me.

Meanwhile, Harvie and I had our future to consider, too. Towards the end of 1998, he suffered a major setback following another accident. This calamity happened when he went to meet some friends for a meal. Approaching the restaurant, he saw his friends through the floor-to-ceiling-height window. As he went to give them a hearty, excitable wave, he slipped on the wet grass and crashed through the glass. He lacerated his wrist and forearm and had to undergo immediate surgery to repair his shredded ligaments and tendons, and salvage the use of his right hand.

The accident put a stop to Harvie's roofing work, which was a blessing. In fact, he couldn't work for a few months as I played Florence Nightingale at home. It was awful for him; he couldn't make a cup of tea, he couldn't dress himself or cut up his food unaided, and he had to learn to write again.

But by summer 1999, after many rehab and occupational therapy sessions, he was thankfully back to his usual, healthy self.

Things really picked up for Harvie and me then. I'd just started a new role at Procter & Gamble, working as a marketing assistant for their Fine Fragrances department.

I loved everything about my new job – the high-end brands, the glamour and, of course, the smells. Working in this field reminded me of the days when I'd admired the elegant assistants in Rackhams department store and dreamed of a career as a beauty journalist. I liaised with agencies, briefing them on brand identity for their print ads in glossy magazines. I'd make frequent trips into London to study how our Fine Fragrances were displayed in department stores. One of my favourite projects was to help develop the 'personality' of the perfume, G by Giorgio Beverly Hills. I worked on how we described the aroma – the top notes of melon, pineapple, and grape, with middle notes of peony, orchid, peach and ginger, the fragrance based with warm sandalwood and vetiver. I was in my element.

In early August, Harvie landed a great job too, as a training and business development manager for the Swedish home appliance manufacturer, Electrolux. He was delighted; finally, he felt he was on a 'career path' with great prospects – and a company car to boot.

Those were exciting days for us as a couple. Our bond was unbreakable as we thrived, professionally and romantically. We loved each other to bits and not one day passed that we didn't feel truly blessed that the universe had brought us together.

We frequently talked about our future: where we wanted to live, getting married and the possibility of having children. I remember a beautiful conversation we had one evening, soon after Harvie had received his job offer.

We were sitting at the dining table, tucking into a meal of salmon and roasted vegetables, cooked by Harvie, Eva Cassidy's 'Songbird' playing in the background. Clinking our wine glasses with a celebratory 'cheers', Harvie said, 'Finally, I can contribute. I'm going to work my way up at Electrolux and we'll be able to buy our own house, get married and think about starting a family perhaps.'

I smiled, then the dream I'd carried since my childhood slipped from my lips. 'I wonder what our kids will be like. I've always wanted a baby girl. When I was younger, my mum told me I looked like Grace Kelly, so I imagined that my birth mother must look like her. It was all a bit of a fairy tale, but I decided that if I was lucky enough to one day have a baby daughter, I'd absolutely name her Grace.'

Harvie put down his knife and fork and reached for my hand. 'You do look like Grace Kelly!' he said. 'Well, Grace sounds like a beautiful name to me if we have a daughter.'

I squeezed his hand. I couldn't have wished for a happier moment. 'Thank you. I love you Harvs.'

Harvie raised his glass again. 'I love you too, Liz. Here's to us.'

Our glasses chimed, the music played on, and we chatted excitedly, blissfully unaware of the brutal heartache and fear that awaited us.

8

Thank You, Robbie Williams

Englefield Green, Surrey, mid-August 1999
'Hey, stop scrolling.' I nudged Harvie's thigh with my foot. 'I want to see that Robbie Williams advert.' We were in our usual positions on the sofa, me propped against the right arm, feet nestled in Harvie's lap. A typical weeknight in front of the TV.

We'd caught the first couple of seconds of the advert, which featured a montage of close-up shots of various bikini-clad women on a beach, before cutting to a scene which showed Robbie zooming out to sea on a jet ski.

'Right, let's see what Robbie's up to.' Harvie, an incorrigible channel-hopper, pointed the remote control at the TV, and Robbie reappeared on the screen. 'Look, he's wearing fake boobs!'

We giggled at first at cheeky-faced Robbie. He was now standing on the shoreline, sporting swimming shorts and a pointy pair of pretend breasts, waves crashing behind him. His message was serious, though.

Robbie cupped his crotch. 'Eh, if you men paid more attention to these,' he said, suggesting his testicles, 'instead of these,' he said, as he grabbed his strap-on boobs and stepped right up to the camera so his face filled the screen, 'then maybe fewer of us would be dying of testicular cancer – so go and check 'em out.' The whooshing sea sound continued with the next frame, which displayed the phone number for the Everyman Male Cancer Campaign. The final shot showed Robbie in a wetsuit and life vest sans his faux boobs getting off the jet ski. 'Did you get it?' he shouts, running up the shore towards the camera, arms aloft in a ta-da gesture.

The advert ended and Harvie continued channel-hopping: a few minutes of *Men Behaving Badly* morphed into *Bremner, Bird and Fortune*, but Robbie's testicular cancer advert stuck in my mind. I said to Harvie, 'It's really good that Robbie's involved in that campaign. There's so much awareness about breast cancer – we're encouraged to check our boobs regularly – but I don't suppose men think to examine their balls. Do you check yours?'

Harvie looked at me with raised brows. 'No, not really, but I've never noticed anything weird down there.' He massaged my feet, grinning now. 'Anyway, if there was anything wrong with my balls, you would've noticed.'

'That's true, but you probably should check them, just to be safe. It's important.' Unlike my adoptive parents, I had no problem with open discussions, especially where medical matters were concerned.

'Yeah, I suppose. Don't worry though, I'm young, fit, and healthy – as far as I'm aware.'

We spoke no more about the advert or Harvie's balls that night. The next morning, we followed our normal routine: I got up at 7 a.m., leaving Harvie to carry on sleeping – he was due to start his new job at Electrolux on 1 September – had my first coffee of the day, ate breakfast, showered then went downstairs to make a drink for Harvie, who'd just woken up.

Like clockwork, he drank his coffee in bed, then went for a shower while I flitted around the bedroom, getting ready for work.

I was sitting at the dressing table, putting on my make-up when Harvie returned to the bedroom, naked but for a towel sarong. 'Any plans for today, darling?' I asked, speaking to his reflection in the dressing-table mirror.

He sat down on the end of the bed behind me. 'Erm, about that Robbie Williams ad – you know what we were saying last night, about checking my balls, well ...'

I turned to face him. 'What's the matter, Harvs?'

'I'm fine,' he said, although he looked confused, 'but I did check, twice – once last night when I went to the loo, then again just now in the shower – and I've found a lump – and I don't think it should be there.'

'Where? Let me have a feel,' I said, trying not to panic. At twenty-two, Harvie was strong and sporty and, aside from being accident-prone like me, was rarely unwell. *Hopefully, this is nothing to worry about*, I thought as Harvie unwrapped the towel from his waist and stood up beside me.

'It's just here,' he said, guiding my hand to the underside of his right testicle. 'I'm sure it's nothing, but ...'

I immediately felt the lump. It was small and hard, like a hazelnut, unmoving when I gently pressed it. A lump that most definitely shouldn't be there. 'Darling, you need to get that looked at by a doctor straight away. You can't leave this.' I was seriously worried.

'Maybe it's a cyst or something,' Harvie replied, grabbing his towel off the bed. He kissed my head. 'But don't worry, I'll call the GP, get an appointment. I'm sure it's nothing serious – I mean, I feel fine – I haven't felt unwell at all.'

I went to work and Harvie booked a doctor's appointment for that afternoon. I couldn't concentrate all day for worrying. *Please don't let there be anything wrong with him. What if that lump is something serious, cancerous ... I can't lose him.* I couldn't eat a thing, my stomach churning with nerves. When 4 p.m. came, the time of Harvie's appointment, I was beside myself, but trying to think positively, his words from that morning replaying in my mind: 'I'm sure it's nothing serious – I mean, I feel fine – I haven't felt unwell at all.'

Our house phone rang out when I called it at 5 p.m. *Maybe that's a good sign,* I reasoned. *Harvie must be out and about, gone to play football after his appointment, maybe. He probably would have called me at work if there was cause for alarm.*

Harvie was in the kitchen when I got home, a pasta dish on the go. 'Well, how did you get on at your appointment?' I said, as he bent to kiss me.

'I don't want to worry you,' he said, looking concerned himself. 'The doctor said they'll need to investigate the lump. He said it was a matter of urgency – but he did say try not to worry, so ...'

I stared at him for a moment, immediately picturing the worst-case scenario. I wrapped my arms around his waist and looked up at him, trying not to cry or let the terror show on my face. 'We'll be alright,' I said.

Harvie smiled. 'Of course we will. Even if the lump is cancerous, I'm young. I've found it early – thanks to you wanting to watch that Robbie Williams ad. I probably wouldn't have bothered checking myself if we hadn't had that conversation last night. If it does turn out to be cancer, I can get treatment. I'm going to be absolutely fine. I'm tough as old boots.' This was typical of Harvie, he had a ridiculously positive mindset; he always saw the best in people and situations.

I nodded, and said through the tears I could no longer stop, 'I know, darling. I know.'

* * *

The next two weeks were a bit of a blur; I was worried sick. I knew Harvie was concerned too, but he didn't really show it – I think he was more worried about how *I* felt, bless him.

Everything happened so fast – scarily fast. Just ten days after we'd discovered the lump, Harvie was called to St Peter's Hospital in Chertsey, Surrey, to undergo a biopsy. We were, of course, anxious about what this procedure might reveal, but equally relieved to know the matter was being investigated promptly.

I went to the hospital with Harvie that morning. We had a comical moment when he changed out of his clothes and put on an NHS surgical gown and stockings. The gown was way too small for his 6-foot 4-inch frame. He looked like a giant wearing a tiny doll's dress.

The nurses on the ward were lovely – friendly and chatty. We were so grateful to them for putting us at ease. I think they warmed to us because we were young – and smiley. Smiling and laughing at Harvie in his gown, which was flapping at the back, helped us to cope with the situation a little.

When the time came for Harvie to go into theatre, I walked with him as far as I was allowed to go – out of the ward, through a small labyrinth of pale-blue, antiseptic-scented corridors, and up to the door that gave way to the anaesthesia room. I hugged him tight, hearing his steady heartbeat as I rested the side of my face on his gowned chest. 'I love you, Harvs,' I said. 'I'll be here when you come back.'

'I love you too. Try not to worry. At least we're in the right place to get it sorted.' Harvie kissed me goodbye, then turned to the nurse who'd accompanied us. 'Okay, let's do this,' he said, and my heart went out to him as I watched him walk into that room, his broad shoulders pulled back, head held high, huge and strong, yet vulnerable in his ill-fitting gown.

I went back to the ward and waited for what felt like an age in the seat beside Harvie's bed. It was a men-only ward, at full capacity. Racked with anxiety, I couldn't sit still, wondering how the biopsy was going. I didn't dare leave my seat in case Harvie came back. *When* will *he be back?*

A man in the bed next to Harvie's caught my gaze. He lifted his hand, attached to a drip, and gave me a wave and a friendly smile. He must've seen how nervous I was – I kept fidgeting, biting the insides of my cheeks, picking at the skin around my fingernails. I smiled back at him, appreciative of his kindness. *Keep smiling, we'll get through this.*

Eventually, one of the nurses we'd met earlier came over to say that Harvie was now in the recovery room. 'Don't worry,' she assured me, 'he'll be back with you very soon.'

I shot out of my chair as he appeared from around the corner of the ward, another friendly nurse pushing him in a wheelchair. 'You're back,' I whispered, as he levered himself out of the chair.

I helped him into bed, then dragged my chair close to him, sat down and held his hand. He was still groggy, but he gave me a sleepy-eyed smile. 'How're you?' he said.

I smiled. Typical Harv. 'Never mind me. How do *you* feel? Are you in pain?'

'I'm fine. Just a bit tired, but I'll be alright.'

The nurse unhooked a clipboard from the foot of the bed. 'I take it this lovely young lady is your girlfriend,' she said to Harvie, tilting her head in my direction.

'Yes,' he said, 'This is Liz.'

'Well, lovely to meet you, Liz,' she said. 'My name's Sally. Now, we need to have a little chat about your operation, Daniel. Do you want Liz to stay for this?' It sounded alien hearing Harvie's first name.

'Yes,' he replied, rolling his head across the pillow to look at me. 'Of course.'

Sally pulled the curtains, enclosing us in a tiny tent-like space, then she sat down on the other side of the bed, facing me. She looked at us both for a few seconds, rolling her lips inwards, then she spoke – slowly and softly. 'Daniel, I'm sorry to tell you that the surgeon had to remove the entire testicle.' My eyes met Harvie's, and we froze. She allowed us time to process this unexpected news.

Sally rose. 'I know this isn't what you were expecting to hear, Daniel. I'll give you and Liz some time alone. The surgeon will come to see you shortly. He'll explain what happens next, what your options are. Would you both like a nice cup of tea?'

'That'll be lovely. Thanks, Sally,' I said, and she disappeared with a humble swish of the curtain.

I don't remember much about the chunk of time before the surgeon arrived. We were both in shock.

The surgeon popped his head around the curtain. 'Daniel, how're you doing now?' he said. I guessed he was in his mid-forties.

'Yeah, I'm not bad, thanks,' Harvie lied. I knew this news had hit him hard.

'So, yes,' began the surgeon. His warm voice belied his clinical appearance. 'I'm afraid I had to remove the testicle, young man.'

'I understand,' said Harvie. Then, with a woozy wink at me, added, 'At least I've still got my other one.'

'We had to remove the entire testicle because it was clear the lump was a malignant tumour – it was the safest option. A

137

biopsy would have injured your testicle, and then there's a risk of the cancer spreading to the scrotum ...'

Hearing those words – cancer, malignant tumour – was a huge shock, to say the least. Our life together as we knew it was turned upside down in that moment.

'I'll be referring you to the oncology team. They'll arrange further scans to make sure the cancer hasn't spread to other parts of the body, and will determine the course of action from there. Okay, Daniel?'

We were absolutely not okay. We were distraught. My limbs turned hollow. Any everyday worries we'd had until now felt meaningless, unimportant. I tried to hide my fear at the prospect of losing him, loss having been ingrained in me from the very moment I was born, an intrinsic presence in my life. I thought to myself, *Surely he can't be taken from me too?* But, of course, my fear remained unspoken, as I recalled again, *Keep smiling, We'll get through this.*

We thanked the surgeon, and off he went, cutting a ghostly figure in his white lab coat as he slipped between the curtains. Harvie looked at me, a weak smile trembling across his strong face. 'We'll get through this, sweetheart. I did some research on testicular cancer the other day. Apparently, if the cancer hasn't spread, the survival rate in men of my age is 99 per cent.'

'We'll get through this together,' I said, smiling back at him. Inside, I crumbled to pieces.

* * *

The atmosphere on the ward shifted dramatically when a few of Harvie's mates – including his best friends Matt and Tony – visited later that afternoon. We heard them before we saw them. 'Wotcher, Harvs,' they hollered in unison.

Harvie relayed to his friends what the surgeon had told us. 'I've lost one of my boys,' he said with a brave laugh, 'but I'll be fine. Hopefully the cancer hasn't spread. I'll get it treated, then I'll be good to go.'

'Yeah, you'll be alright, Harvs,' said Matt. 'You'll be flying a jumbo jet on one engine, but ...' We all burst out laughing at that. More jokes followed: 'A bird in the hand is worth two in the bush'; 'You're firing on one cylinder' and so on. Within minutes we were in hysterics, and Harvie was back, laughing with the lads, all teasing one another, as they do. The boys lifted us with their humour.

They really rallied round, too, assuring us that we had their full support. 'You'll get through this,' they said. *Keep smiling, stay strong* – that would be our mantra from now on, we decided. Although maintaining this mindset would prove challenging throughout the months ahead.

Harvie's diagnosis coincided with him starting at Electrolux. It must've been so difficult for him, calling his new boss and telling her, 'I've just been diagnosed with testicular cancer, which I need treatment for. I realise this might be inconvenient.' But his boss was brilliant about it – she told Harvie he should start the job and could take as much time off work as he needed.

Examination of Harvie's removed testicle revealed that the tumour was indeed malignant. So, scan after scan, after watching and waiting, the sense of being in limbo and at the mercy of this disease took its toll. Physically for Harvie, and emotionally for both of us.

Fortunately, the cancer hadn't spread, but his oncologist said he would need four intensive cycles of chemotherapy to prevent the cancer returning.

Before his treatment started, we had another appointment with his oncologist, who outlined the chemotherapy process and the likely side-effects of the drug, which included hair loss, tiredness, sickness, weight gain from steroids and … infertility. 'I'm not sure whether you're thinking about starting a family, but you might want to consider banking your sperm. Chemotherapy can leave some men infertile,' the oncologist told us.

This was another devastating blow. We hadn't even thought about this as we faced the trauma of Harvie's diagnosis. Now we were effectively being told we might not be able to have children.

The dream of my baby Grace was fading, disappearing like smoke, and to this day I can still recall the pain of this news. My yearning to be a mother was so strong, burning inside of me for as long as I could remember – the desperate desire to see my features in somebody else's face, to recognise myself in another human being, to share mannerisms, quirks, *genes*. The chance of having true, real, biological connections taken away from me was almost too much to bear. I held Harvie's hand. 'Our main priority is that he gets fit and well again. That the cancer doesn't come back,' I said.

Harvie and I agreed to bank his sperm. 'We do want to start a family one day,' he told the oncologist.

After his appointment at the sperm clinic, he rang me at work and told me how awkward and undignified the process was. *Keep smiling, stay strong,* I recalled once again.

Looking back, it astonishes me how we coped. During this time, my communication with Yvonne came to a standstill. Emotionally, I felt I couldn't focus on our relationship. I was beginning to feel stuck between two families, trying to manage two sets of emotions – conscious of Yvonne's hurt and regret, while also considering my adoptive parents' feelings. I spoke to Jenny, explaining that I needed to take a break in the contact with Yvonne, just for a while. My sole priority at that point was Harvie as he faced his first round of chemo.

I had to attend an off-site training course for work on the day of Harvie's first chemotherapy treatment at St Luke's Cancer Centre at Royal Surrey Hospital. Sadly, this meant I couldn't be with him until my course finished, when I'd head directly to the hospital.

Harvie set off to his appointment in my Vauxhall Nova – only he didn't make it to the hospital. He called me from the scene of the crash on the M25.

'Before you start panicking, I just want you to know that I'm okay. I've had a bit of an accident but I'm still in one piece,' he said. It frightened the life out of me when he explained what had happened. He was lucky to be alive after his 'bit of an accident'. The driver of a Dutch lorry hadn't seen Harvie overtaking him when he pulled into the middle lane at 50 mph – then hit Harvie's rear passenger side. The car spun around and became wedged beneath the front of the lorry, pushing it some distance along the M25. 'The police said it was incredibly lucky that I got stuck under the lorry,' added Harvie. 'Otherwise, the car could have flipped and rolled, and the outcome could've been very different. I banged my head on the window on impact, but I'm totally fine. Anyway, they're recovering the car, and I'm getting a lift back. I'll need to call the hospital and change my appointment.'

I immediately left my course – I had to see for myself that Harvie was okay. I met him in The Happy Man, where he was nursing a whisky to calm his nerves. 'Sorry about the car,' he said, 'but there's not too much damage, considering.'

'Thank God you're okay, I've been worried sick.' I kissed his bruised forehead. 'And never mind the bloody car.'

* * *

Over the next three months, the St Luke's Cancer Centre, based in Guildford's Royal Surrey Hospital, became our second home as Harvie underwent chemo treatment. In true Harvie style, he remained positive throughout each cycle, but it was harrowing to watch him go through this gruelling therapy.

I'd be there with him as often as I could, work allowing. The chemo made him nauseous and tired, but he made such an effort to ensure that we had quality time when we were together.

I tried to be as strong as Harvie, to be upbeat during my visits, even when I was on the brink of being overcome with emotion and tears. Sometimes, Harvie had to stay overnight at St Luke's, and I hated leaving him there when visiting time ended. I'd walk across the almost empty, floodlit car park, tears streaming down my face. So many times, I thought, *I'm going to lose him. I can't lose him.*

Beneath our let's-be-positive-and-smile-through-this outlook lurked the terrifying reality that his cancer could return, that the chemo might not work. I didn't voice my fears to Harvie; he was so stoic. 'You make sure you look after yourself, sweetheart,' he'd say when I kissed his moon face goodbye at the cancer centre. (The steroids bloated him terribly.) 'Get plenty of rest – and make sure you're eating properly. Don't worry about me, I'm going to be fine.' Honestly, I can't begin to describe the love and admiration I felt for him in those moments.

Poor Harvie. He would still go to work as much as was physically possible between his chemo sessions, but I could see the toll the treatment was taking on him. On days when he was too poorly to go to work, he'd lie on the sofa, listening to music and drifting off to sleep. I'd watch him, his presence still large, yet he seemed so vulnerable. The chemo gave him horrendous mouth ulcers, red and craterous. He was exhausted and, as expected, he started to lose his hair. It fell out like needles dropping from a Christmas tree; he had only to touch his head and dozens of blond strands would float to the floor. He managed to retain some of his hair for his sister Louise's wedding in early December 1999. After that, Harvie decided to shave his hair off. I can still picture it now: Harvie, kneeling over the bath as I ran the electric razor over his head, the pale gleam of his skin, the shape of his naked skull. 'I wonder what it'll grow back like,' he mused. 'Thicker, probably,' I said, my throat straining as I tried not to cry.

Harvie was in his final three-week cycle of chemo then, but once that ended, we'd have to wait at least eight weeks before his next scan to see whether the cancer had returned. A whole two months, of agonising waiting, while we both tried to somehow carry on – me going to work, taking care of him, and Harvie doing whatever he could manage in between his treatments.

Christmas was tough; we didn't spend the holiday together. On 23 December, Harvie headed to his parents, Margy and Wayne's house in Howsham, North Lincolnshire, and I went back to Harborne. I was pleased that Harvie would be spending some much-needed quality time with his lovely mum and dad, but equally, I couldn't bear for us to be apart.

We set off on our respective journeys home, me in my little red Nova, Harvie at the wheel of the van from his roofing days. We drove in convoy, Harvie taking the lead, until the North and The Midlands beckoned, forcing us apart on separate motorways. I waved at his van, and he blinked his hazard lights and waved back, then I watched him disappear into the distance, towards the North. I cried on and off during my lonely drive to Birmingham, cheery Christmas songs keeping me company. I missed him so much already.

By New Year's Eve, Harvie had finished his chemo. He said he felt more energised, less tired than he had been, for sure. We still didn't know whether the treatment had been successful, but we remained hopeful.

We saw in the millennium with friends – at The Happy Man, of course. Harvie still had his bald head, bless him. It was a poignant evening for us; we'd been through so much distress over the past few months.

Just before midnight, Robbie Williams's 'Angels' played over the pub's sound system. My heart jolted. Harvie and I shared a knowing look, a look of realisation, prompting a flurry of *what ifs*. I said to him, 'It feels like a millennium ago when we first saw that advert. What if we hadn't have seen it? What if you hadn't checked your balls? Where would we be now? What …' I welled up then.

'Well, it's thanks to you – and Robbie – that I *did* check my balls,' said Harvie, enveloping me in one of his wonderful bear hugs. 'Anyway, more importantly, I need another drink. Let's forget about it, just for tonight, and enjoy ourselves.'

The song came to an end and the countdown began, everyone, us included, chanting, 'Ten, nine, eight, seven, six, five, four, three, two, one.' Big Ben's stately bongs chimed from the wall-mounted television, and the room erupted with cheers. Harvie's lips, full and warm, connected with mine. 'Happy New Year, my love,' we said together.

Then Harvie pulled back his shoulders, slapped his bald head, as he did now and then, just because the silly side of him was still very much present, and said, 'You know, I think I'm going to be just fine.'

I smiled. *Keep smiling, stay strong.*

9

In Sickness and in Health

The new millennium brought us good fortune.

In March, Harvie went for a scan, which showed that the cancer hadn't returned. His oncologist didn't tell him, 'You're in the clear,' or, 'You're in remission' – he would have to go for regular tests for the next five years before that could be confirmed. But we were so relieved to hear that the chemotherapy had been successful. No further cycles were necessary.

Harvie's cancer was traumatic for us as a young couple. Without doubt, his strength, dignity and positivity carried us through those testing months. He didn't witness my breakdowns during his overnight stays in hospital, when I'd curl up in a ball in our bed, saying to myself again and again, 'Please, *please* let him recover from this. I can't live without him.' I barely ate – my appetite vanishes when I'm anxious – and I couldn't sleep properly. I was an emotional mess.

We were a solid couple before Harvie's diagnosis, but his illness strengthened our bond even further. Getting through those desperate months together, only four months into our relationship, made us appreciate how precious life is, and how lucky we were to have one another. We both knew we wanted to be together forever.

Harvie was beginning to look more like his former self, aside from his hair, which grew back curly, in a darker shade of birch-brown. Whenever he came home from playing football, I'd hug him and gratefully breathe in his sweaty odour that was tangible evidence of his life force.

At last, things were returning to normal, but we'd never take anything for granted again. We valued every shared moment, our home, our jobs, and we appreciated being able to spend time with other people more. As we settled back into our routine, I thought about Yvonne, and decided that now was the time to reconnect with her, to explain my hiatus in communication. It didn't feel right to call her out of the blue, so I wrote her this letter:

Dear Yvonne,

I hope this letter finds you well.

I'm sure this letter will come as a surprise considering our last correspondence was some time ago. I first want to explain my reasons for not maintaining contact for all this time, and I hope that you can understand.

Everything moved quite fast for me after we first made contact. I felt a lot was covered in our letters and calls which was, I guess, good in a way. Personally, there were/are many questions that I needed answers to in order to put 'me' into perspective. I got some of those answers in what was really a short space of time, and it was a lot to take in.

As I've mentioned before, I had been so curious for many years to see a photograph of my birth parents (particularly my birth mother) that when it finally arrived, I felt so anxious that it was difficult for me to even open the envelope and look at them. When I finally plucked up the courage, I remember staring at them for quite some time. It was so very strange for me to see what you looked like. It also opened a can of worms because I also remember wondering whether I bear any resemblance to my birth father.

Harvie recently pointed out another resemblance: you and I have the same 'traps' (very sloping trapezius muscles from our necks down to our shoulders – something he teases me about and has wondered where they came from).

I realise now that I found exchanging letters and phone calls with you quite overwhelming. I felt there was a lot resting on my shoulders, as it were – having to take into consideration the feelings of my family, of you. I hung back because I wanted to finally make contact with you for the right reasons, not because we were both carried away on emotion after all these years.

I want you to know, however, that I was also very conscious of having 'left' you without any explanation (other than via Jenny). It was even difficult for me to explain to her how it had affected me at the time.

There is also the other issue of there never seeming to be a 'right time' to pursue contact. I hope you don't read this the wrong way, but there was always something pressing/important to deal with. Harvie had testicular cancer in August 1999, which meant an operation and several months of chemotherapy, so that was not a good time for us. I am pleased to say the therapy worked and his cancer has not returned.

Anyhow, I now feel in a more positive frame of mind about things, so I think that now is a good time, for me, anyway, to start up contact again. How do you feel about this?

As I said before, I hope that you can understand my various reasons for the lack of contact, and that I still don't want to rush into us meeting in person before we are both ready – for both of our sakes. I thought we could go back to writing to one another and speaking on the phone – we'll see how we both feel.

> Again, I hope this letter finds you, and Martin, well.
> Hope to hear from you soon,
> Liz

As I put the letter in the post I did wonder, *What if my lack of contact had hurt Yvonne? What if she doesn't reply?* That fear of rejection ate away at me again. It reminded me of the first time I'd tentatively reached out to her, with no idea how I'd be received. The same uncertainty and apprehension tormented me. *Will she still be there?*

Yvonne did reply, swiftly as ever, and she was incredibly understanding of my situation:

> Like you, I also found that receiving your letters was quite overwhelming, and I cried when I read them. I'm sorry if you felt pressured in any way – that is not how I wanted you to feel.
>
> When you stopped writing I felt very hurt and upset. I thought, what have I done to hurt or upset you? But I can understand exactly how you were feeling at the time.
>
> I was sorry to hear that Harvie had testicular cancer, but I'm glad to hear that he has recovered.
>
> I'm glad that you now feel more positive about things. I understand totally that you still don't want to rush things, and I certainly don't want you to feel pressurised in any way at all. Like I've said all along, whatever you want to do, however you want to do things, I will go along with it.

Reading Yvonne's letter, I realised that I'd missed hearing her voice, her rounded handwriting that slanted slightly to the left. The internet was now accessible, so Yvonne had added her email address at the end of her letter, but I preferred letter-writing. It felt traditional, nostalgic, and I found her little diversions from our situation comforting and homely: 'Martin has just passed his HGV 2 driving test and is now hoping to get a job driving, as it is what he wants to do.'

Soon, Yvonne and I were in regular contact again, exchanging letters and phone calls as the months went by.

We spoke again about the days following my birth, and with each conversation new information emerged. Yvonne told me how she'd tried to 'work out' how she could keep me while she was in hospital. She said, 'Social Services were absolutely useless. I tried speaking to somebody at the Citizens Advice Bureau, but they weren't helpful. All that was going through my head was, *how can I keep this baby and survive?* I wish I'd found a way.'

It must've been so hard for Yvonne being in that ward with three other women who were able to keep their babies. She recalled hearing those newborns crying through the night. 'I'd wake up and think, *What if Claire's crying in the nursery? Why can't I go to her? Why can't I have my baby with me at night?*' she said.

One day, one of the other mums, Linda, asked Yvonne, 'Why do they keep taking your baby away?'

Yvonne burst into tears. 'I'm not allowed to keep my baby. They're making me give her up for adoption – because I'm not married.'

Linda hugged her then. 'I feel awful now, that we've all got our babies and you can't keep yours. I'm so sorry,' she said.

To this day, I'm shocked and appalled at how I was separated from Yvonne during the night. Newborn babies *need* their mothers – it was barbaric that they did that to us. I was also appalled that my birth father was turned away from the hospital, banned from seeing me before I was taken away for good. It was despicable that the nurse held me up at the nursery window for Yvonne's parents to see – kept at a distance behind the glass, like I was diseased, a danger, not to be approached, like an animal at some kind of zoo exhibit. I still feel this meant that I wasn't worthy of being welcomed, visited, celebrated. Any chance of bonding was controlled. I had arrived in this world and was causing complications from day one. That never leaves you.

One evening, as we chatted over the phone, I asked Yvonne about her feelings towards my adoptive parents: 'You must've wondered who they were, what they were like?'

Yvonne sighed down the phone. 'I never stopped thinking about you after they took you away from me, Liz. I remember praying that you'd gone to a good home, that you were being well looked after. But there was a lot of resentment on my part. I felt robbed of every experience that should have been mine: your first words, watching you grow up, birthday parties … everything. I was very jealous of those people.

'I didn't know whether your new family would tell you about your adoption. Obviously, they did tell you, and it breaks my heart to picture you, reading those documents as a teenager, seeing all those untruths in black and white. You must've thought I just threw you on the pile.'

It was hard to imagine how different my childhood would've been had I stayed with my birth mother. Even now, I ask myself, *Would I be the person I am today if Yvonne had brought me up?* That question was simply impossible to answer, but I understood where Yvonne was coming from regarding my adoptive family. It must've been torturous for her, knowing two strangers were nurturing her baby. She must've felt like this was her punishment – just for having a child out of wedlock. I was, as Yvonne said, robbed from her, taken against her wishes, then 'chosen' by my parents. That's inconceivable, absurd, inhumane. Yvonne and I would share a deep-rooted, everlasting sadness for our lost decades, never knowing 'what could've been'.

Although we were taking things slowly, we were inevitably curious to discover more about each other: our likes and dislikes and, of course, our pasts – to fill in the gaps in our years apart.

I told Yvonne about my childhood; I described how I'd scrutinise my face in the mirror, looking for her, seeking Grace Kelly after Mum said I resembled her. 'I'd look for you in the street,' I said. 'I'd look at every blonde-haired, blue- or green-eyed woman and think, *Could that be her? My birth mother?*'

I explained my strained relationship with Mum, the controlling environment I grew up in, and how my parents never engaged with me regarding my adoption. 'Mentally, I struggled a lot growing up,' I said. 'My parents swept my adoption under the carpet. They told me they'd "chosen" me. My life at home was stifling at times. I felt I couldn't connect with my parents, especially Mum.'

Yvonne also spoke about her past, in which she'd endured untold grief. She had only three remaining blood relatives: me, her aunt Dorothy (her mum's sister) and Dorothy's daughter, Charlotte, who lived in Essex. Yvonne was close to her cousin growing up but didn't see much of her after she moved to Northampton. 'I did think about fleeing to Essex with you,' she told me. 'But I knew Charlotte couldn't help me, and Dorothy was a nasty piece of work. Plus, I couldn't leave Mum alone with Dad – he really was a pig.'

Sadly, Yvonne's mother passed away in 1983. Her father died thirteen years later. The death of her mother and her father's bitterness deeply affected Yvonne: 'I adored my mum. I cried non-stop when she died, and I know it sounds like a horrible thing to say, but I still wish Dad had gone before her.

After Mum passed away, I thought maybe Dad and I might mend our relationship a bit. Well, that never happened. He remained as pig-headed as ever, right up until he died of a stroke in 1996. I didn't grieve for him in the same way as I did for Mum. She was a kind, gentle person. I still miss her today, with all my heart.'

Yvonne had married twice. Her first marriage, to 'Terry', didn't work out: 'Let's just say he was a bit of a mummy's boy. We couldn't go anywhere without Terry's mum tagging along. She interfered in our marriage something terrible, which led to our divorce.'

Bill, Yvonne's second husband, subjected her to unthinkable torment and violence. As she narrates:

He had a temper, Bill. I thought perhaps his anger stemmed from his days serving in the army during 'The Troubles' in Northern Ireland.

I was smitten in the early days of our marriage – and desperate for a child, a baby girl. Bill had wanted a child too, but, as you know, that wasn't to be. I had an ectopic pregnancy, then the infertility treatment failed. I'd already lost you, Liz, and now, to find out I couldn't have another baby … that shattered me. And to think I actually felt guilty for not being able to give Bill children.

He didn't seem to care much about my loss, the selfish so-and-so that he was. He constantly lied to me, and he drank heavily. I'm talking pints of lager first thing in the morning. And he'd turn after drinking, horribly so. He became violent. More than once he had me by the throat, my feet off the floor – I was petrified, too frightened to even scream in case that further antagonised him. I could have had him done for rape a few times, I'm telling you.

I walked on eggshells at home, not knowing when he'd next flip – anything I said or did could set him off, and I always had to keep my car keys in my pocket, ready to escape at any given moment – if I could escape.

Then, in September 1990, Bill disappeared; he went off with his fancy woman he'd been seeing on the side. I came back from work one day to an empty house. He'd taken most of my furniture – only the bed was left.

The woman who Bill ran off with had two kids. Well, he soon decided it wasn't so green on the other side. He called me in December. 'I'm sorry,' he said. 'I want to come home. We can try again. You're the one that I really love.'

I told him, 'No, Bill. You've made your bed,' but he wouldn't take no for an answer. He was like a dog with a bone, calling me every day, begging for a second chance at our marriage. Argh, and eventually, I gave in. Just before Christmas, I took him back – the idiot that I am.

Things were a bit better than before when Bill returned, but it wasn't a good relationship by any stretch of the imagination. I was still anxious and jumpy around him. He'd get up late in the mornings then start boozing, while I was at work. I'd call him on my lunch break every day, just to check he was okay. He was nearly always in a drunken state, slurring down the phone.

One Wednesday lunchtime – 16 January 1991 – Bill didn't answer my call. I had a gut feeling that something wasn't right, so I kept calling the house phone, all afternoon. Still, he didn't answer. It was strange; he had virtually no money, so he couldn't go anywhere.

When I got home that evening, there were no lights on. I walked into the pitch-black hallway and called out his name. Silence. There were two switches for the landing light – one at the bottom of the stairs, one at the top. I'd always flick the bottom switch whenever I headed upstairs, but in my haste, I didn't do that this time. I hurried up the stairs, switched on the light, and walked right into Bill, who was hanging by a noose from the loft hatch, his eyes wide and frozen in his blue face, his dead face.

I screamed, then ran downstairs, flew out of the front door in my stockinged feet to our neighbours across the road, Scott and Maureen. 'Please help me!' I said, shaking with shock. 'Bill's committed suicide in the house.'

Scott came back with me. He lifted Bill down while I called the police. I wasn't the same after Bill killed himself, in my home. I thought, I must've done something really bad in my life to deserve this. I couldn't sleep upstairs for seven months afterwards, haunted by flashbacks. Every time I went upstairs, I could still see him in my mind, hanging from the loft. Why did he have to kill himself in the house, knowing I'd come home to find him there?

I felt Bill's presence everywhere in that house. Eventually, I had to move.

Yvonne relayed that harrowing story to me during one of our phone calls. It horrified me that she'd endured so much undeserved violence in her life. I heard the vulnerability and fear in her voice, trembling occasionally, her pauses between sentences as she fought back tears.

Fortunately, Martin seemed like a good man. He and Yvonne were inseparable. 'Oh, we'd be lost without each other,' she said, and this resonated with me; Harvie and I felt the same way.

* * *

The year passed quickly and soon we were welcoming 2001. I had a lot to be grateful for. Now in a more positive headspace, I felt more confident sharing aspects of my life with Yvonne via our phone calls and letters. She was always interested to know what I'd been up to, and I enjoyed hearing her news. Granted, we could never replace those missing years, or get over the grief of being separated after my birth, but we were building a better understanding of each other and our emotions.

Harvie was in good health and flourishing at work – he'd recently been promoted to regional sales manager. I was so proud of him.

In January, Harvie and I got engaged. I'd always dreamed of the fairy-tale proposal, of him getting down on one knee and popping the question as he opened a heart-shaped box holding a diamond ring, but it didn't happen quite like that. A romantic fanfare seemed unnecessary; we were just so happy with each other – I didn't need the fantasy proposal. Everything I had ever wanted and needed was right there. I wanted to experience the genuine emotions of our commitment, celebrate the true love we had for each other, without frills. That's what our engagement signified to me.

We went shopping for an engagement ring together and chose a simple square, princess-cut diamond. It was beautiful. Harvie still wanted to do the chivalrous thing and ask for Dad's permission to marry me though, so we headed to Birmingham.

I suspected Mum and Dad would be pleased to hear our news. When Harvie and I first got together, Mum had some reservations about who, if anybody, would be good enough for me – but perhaps this is a 'normal' parental response. Her mood changed when Harvie started working for Electrolux. No longer was he a roofer; he had a 'proper' job with a big company, so he looked good on paper now from Mum's perspective.

Dad got along well with Harvie. They often went to football matches together, and, whenever we stayed over at my parents' house, the pair of them would drink whisky in the evenings and chat about business and investment ideas. Dad genuinely enjoyed his company.

Harvie waited for the right moment to speak to Dad, after we'd eaten a simple evening meal of baked beans on toast. 'Shall we sit in the lounge for a bit?' Harvie asked Dad as Mum and I cleared the table. *This is it*, I thought. *He's going to ask Dad for my hand in marriage – in the lounge.* At last, those walls and bonneted ladies and little tasselled footstool would witness a happy occasion.

Mum and I stayed in the kitchen while Harvie and Dad disappeared into the lounge. I speedily loaded the dishwasher, trying not to explode with excitement. Mum flitted around, in the zone with her clean-up operation, meticulously wiping the worktops and putting things away, as she always did. I switched on the dishwasher, and it gurgled into life – a mundane sound for a joyous event, I thought.

Dad appeared a few minutes later, beaming at me. 'Can you both come into the lounge please?' I knew exactly what was to follow, but Mum didn't have a clue. Everybody assumed their normal positions – Mum in her chair by the fire, Dad in his, by the mahogany display cabinet and Harvie on the sofa by the door. I sat beside him. At which point he got up, knelt down in front of me and said, 'Liz, will you be my wife?'

'Yes,' I cried. Mum shrieked and clasped her hands. Dad held his arms aloft, beckoning me in for a hug. 'Congratulations, you two,' he said. 'Of course I was going to give my permission – how lovely of him to ask me,' said Dad. I could tell that he really appreciated Harvie's gesture.

'Oh, this is wonderful news,' said Mum, relief evident in her smile. 'Congratulations. Let's crack open a bottle of champagne.'

The lounge buzzed with excited chatter and clinking crystal that evening.

'Elizabeth, I presume you'll be having a church wedding.' Typical Mum. 'Have you decided on bridesmaids yet? We'll have to go out and choose your wedding dress. And you'll get married here, in Harborne, won't you?'

I was too elated to question any of her plans yet …

The ensuing months saw many positive changes in our lives. In April, Harvie and I moved house. We bought a three-bedroom 1930s terraced house in South Road, Englefield Green, with a long, narrow back garden complete with a beautiful lilac tree, herbaceous border, greenhouse and a little shed – we felt settled. Our new house was in a great location, close to Royal Holloway University and a short walk to The Happy Man on Harvest Road. Inside, the décor looked tired – old woodchip wallpaper throughout, and the kitchen needed redoing. We couldn't afford a new kitchen, but we didn't care. This was our first house together, and we absolutely loved it. It was *home*.

Not long after we moved to South Road, Procter & Gamble announced job cuts and plant closures. During this reshuffle, I was told my role would relocate to Geneva. Exciting though this sounded, my heart was in Englefield Green, with Harvie, so I took voluntary redundancy instead.

For the first time, I stopped to consider what I wanted to do for a living. As much as I'd enjoyed marketing, I wanted a change from the corporate world. I never really felt at home in that environment and I wanted to explore what I was passionate about, so I decided to put some of my £4,000 redundancy money towards learning new skills.

I signed up for online courses in complementary therapy, aromatherapy, massage, and Indian head massage. I passed all my written and practical assessments with flying colours, then built a small client base of people who came to the house for treatments. I loved working with my clients, connecting with them, helping them to relax and making them feel special. I loved sending them out of my house in a better headspace than they had come in. I felt I was making a difference to people, and I genuinely adored this work.

Meanwhile, I also began a new job at Hall Grove School, in Bagshot, initially as a class music teacher to pupils aged four to thirteen, then as a teaching assistant, first in Year 1, then in Year 2. This was quite a shift from the marketing world, but I loved interacting with the children, helping them learn and hearing their inquisitive conversations. Some of the children needed that extra bit of help, to have things explained at a slower pace, in a slightly different way perhaps. I loved these sessions – I found that I was good at finding out what each child needed, and how best to connect with them. I felt fulfilled in this job, a much more natural place for me to be. I felt like I was coming home, to myself.

Away from work, Harvie and I had our wedding to arrange. Organising our wedding was my dream come true. I had a lever-arch file which I filled with fabric swatches for bridesmaid dresses, pictures from bridal magazines, wedding stationery samples, names of classic car-hire companies, sample menus and, most importantly, ideas for my dress.

We set the date for our wedding, 3 August 2002, which would take place at St Faith & St Laurence Church in Harborne, followed by a reception at Hilton Birmingham Metropole hotel.

Mum was on her own mission when it came to our wedding plans. She wanted to control everything from the guest list to our cake. Harvie doesn't like fruit cake, so I suggested one tier could be a Victoria sponge. Mum's reaction to that: 'Oh, no, no, no. All tiers *must* be fruit cake. It's traditional. You can't possibly have a Victoria sponge wedding cake.'

'But nobody will *know* what kind of cake it is beneath the icing,' I sighed. Another hard 'no' from Mum. I despaired, her constant need to impress was tiresome, coming above what Harvie and I wanted.

I loved the idea of informal, reportage photography for our big day. I'd admired this style in the many bridal magazines I'd devoured – unposed, unstaged, creative, just natural images. I wanted to capture emotion, feeling, laughter, love, the 'realness' of us. When I suggested this idea to my parents, who'd already commissioned a local wedding photographer, Mum again put her foot down. 'No, Elizabeth. Traditional photos are better.' It was exasperating, stifling.

We even clashed over my dress. I remember going shopping with her in Birmingham one weekend. Wedding-day shopping with your mother should be a rite of passage, a beautiful, memorable experience, but Mum had other ideas.

Sifting through the ivory and white dresses in one bridal shop, I found a lovely boat-necked gown, which was just what I had in mind. It was elegant, with a fitted bodice and train, its neckline stretching from shoulder to shoulder.

Mum's face darkened as I admired the dress. 'Goodness me, no. A bride can't bare her shoulders on her wedding day, you can't be showing all that flesh in a church. You'll look like a slut. Keep looking, Elizabeth.'

I was disgusted at the word she had used. Devastated that such a word had been used to describe what I might look like gliding down the aisle on my wedding day. By my own mother. I wanted this to be my special moment, but I felt like a child again, her making me wear the frilly dresses with their Peter Pan collars.

Mum pooh-poohed many of the dresses I tried on, although I did eventually find one that met her approval – a beautiful, jewel-necked, classic ivory dress, with a full skirt, elegant train and a 1950s'-style bow that sat at the small of my back. I picked a simple veil that fluttered to my waist and a pair of vintage-inspired elbow-length gloves – a nod to Grace Kelly.

'That's more like it,' Mum said, as the shop assistant straightened my train.

I smiled at my reflection in the mirror. 'This is definitely the one.'

* * *

Disagreements with Mum aside, I couldn't wait to marry Harvie. Our wedding day was about us, to celebrate our love and commitment to one another. I loved planning every detail. Music was important to Harvie and me, so we spent a long time deliberating over which pieces to play at our wedding. We chose Charpentier's 'Te Deum' prelude for my entrance into the church, and Widor's triumphantly powerful 'Toccata' from his Organ Symphony No. 5 would play as we began our first walk as a married couple back down the aisle and out of the church.

Another Christmas came and went, spring passed, then before we knew it, our big day was upon us.

I'd told Yvonne about our engagement and wedding plans. 'Oh, you're going to make a beautiful bride, Liz,' she said over the phone the week prior to our wedding. 'Send me some photographs – I'd love to see you in your dress.'

It hadn't occurred to me to invite Yvonne – at that stage we still hadn't met each other. Also, it wouldn't have been fair on Mum and Dad to invite Yvonne to our wedding.

On 3 August 2002, a beautiful, blue-skied sunny day, I walked down the aisle, escorted by Dad, to my brother playing Charpentier's 'Te Deum' prelude on the organ, accompanied by his friend on the trumpet. My bridesmaids – my two close friends, Tasha and Liz – in sugary pink satin gowns, followed us. I'll never forget the moment I reached the altar, when Harvie, so handsome in his dark morning suit, turned to face me. I saw his eyes water as he lifted my veil. My heart and stomach fluttered at once, overcome with emotion.

The church fell silent, then we began our wedding vows. I beamed through most lines – until we reached the 'in sickness and in health' vow. I looked up at Harvie and remembered all that we'd been through, and how often I'd feared losing him. Tears filled my eyes and I had to clear my throat, then affirmed, loud and clear, albeit with a wobble in my voice, 'In sickness and in health.'

10

I'm Home

South Road, Englefield Green, Friday, 1 August 2003
I sat at my dressing table, fingers quivering as I tried to fix the back onto one of my pearl-drop wedding earrings.

'What will I say to her?' I said to Dan, who was rummaging through the wardrobe. 'I'm so nervous. What if it's really awkward?' Since we'd been married, I'd decided to start calling Harvie by his first name – it seemed more appropriate.

It was mid-morning and we were getting ready to leave the house. I was about to meet Yvonne in person for the first time, less than three hours from now. This was a momentous event, one we'd been building up to for almost six years, a moment my body had craved since I was born – to feel my birth mother's arms around me – to smell her, touch her, hear her voice in person, to see how she moved, how she held herself. I was excited, but also terrified at the enormity of what lay ahead.

'What should I wear? I mean, my outfit will be the first thing she sees, it's important,' I added.

Dan pulled a shirt out of the wardrobe. 'It's going to be great. Just be you, sweetheart, and what you wear won't matter.'

I managed to fasten my earring. 'Oh, Dan, that's lovely.'

He always seemed to say the right things at important times. I'd instigated the meeting with Yvonne – and Martin – a few days ago, and told Dan our plan. 'Where on earth should we go?' I'd said. 'No place seems suitable enough for us to meet them for the first time.'

'Leave it with me,' Dan replied, immediately searching online. Within half an hour, he'd booked a courtyard table at The Bear Hotel in Woodstock, the picturesque market town bordering the Cotswolds. The hotel looked stunning – a former thirteenth-century coaching inn, steeped in history and charm with its façade cloaked in ivy, and oak-beamed ceilings inside. It was the perfect setting: cosy, unostentatious.

I tried to picture myself greeting Yvonne in that paved courtyard while I fumbled with my second earring. *Do I hug her? Is it too much, too soon, to hug her?*

Dan buttoned his shirt. 'I'll go and fill up the car, leave you to finish getting ready.' He kissed my head on his way out. 'Try not to worry, it'll be fine.'

I still couldn't decide what to wear. *What will Yvonne be wearing?* I thought as I leafed through the outfits in my wardrobe. *This isn't an occasion for jeans. That black dress is too formal.* It was going to be hot this afternoon, around 25°C according to the forecast. *Maybe a summer dress would be best.*

I stood for ages, sliding the hangers this way and that, pulling out dresses and skirts, tops and blouses, tossing some items onto the bed as 'maybes'. I wanted to look respectful but not intimidating, friendly but not too casual. It was important to me to get this right – it's not every day that you reunite with your birth mother after twenty-nine years.

Finally, I settled on a poppy-red, sleeveless top and a long, dark, flowing skirt patterned with delicate red and pink flowers. Vibrant and inviting, smart but casual. I changed into my chosen outfit, put on my make-up and ran the straighteners through my hair. I kept dropping things, misplacing stuff – *where did I put that mascara?* – I was a nervous wreck.

How will I even greet her?

As we set off for Woodstock, I remembered Jenny's description of the 'reunion' process: 'It can often feel like an emotional rollercoaster. Reunions can bring up a lot of intense feelings from the past. Sometimes, the euphoria of having found one another is replaced by feelings of sadness and loss.'

This was true. I'd felt myriad emotions throughout my communication with Yvonne. My sadness and loss after being taken from her as a baby had never left me – it never will. Although Yvonne and I had already talked at length about my beginnings, and our shared grief, meeting her in the flesh took our reunion to a different plane emotionally. Today, I wouldn't be hearing her voice over the phone, or via her handwriting. I'd actually witness her reactions, responses. You can't script a reunion. This was unknown territory, for both of us.

Driving along the M40, Dan at the wheel, I wondered what was going through Yvonne's mind. *Did she feel nervous too?* I was eight weeks old when she last saw me, when she'd kissed my head for the final time and whispered, *Please forgive me*. She knew then that she might never see her baby again. Soon, I'd be standing before her as a grown woman. I couldn't begin to comprehend how strange that must feel for her.

Notwithstanding our previous communication, Yvonne and I were starting from scratch. As a baby, I'd seen her, but I couldn't recall that memory, whereas Yvonne had experienced all the emotions of carrying me, giving birth, dressing, and feeding me, reading to me – and finally saying goodbye to me. While I acknowledged I was Yvonne's child, I was also aware that I'd lived far away from her and her world for many years. *I hope I don't disappoint her*, I thought.

My stomach flipped when we arrived in Woodstock. There was no going back now. We were here, parking up outside The Bear Hotel, twenty-five minutes before our pre-arranged 1 p.m. meeting. Being late was not an option. I looked at Dan before we got out of the car. 'Please, please don't let her arrive at the same time,' I said.

Dan patted my thigh. 'We're very early. C'mon, let's go and get you a drink. It'll settle your nerves before they arrive.'

'I'm so bloody nervous, Dan.'

We walked into the hotel, and Dan went to the bar while I headed outside to the courtyard, remembering Yvonne's words when we'd arranged our lunch date, our first physical meeting: 'I hate being late, so we'll probably be there before you.'

I stepped outside, blinking in the glaring sunlight, conversations and laughter swirling around me as I passed occupied tables sheltered by parasols. I stopped to shield my eyes, to look for our table, and that's when I saw her, sitting alone on the far right-hand side of the courtyard, leaning into her right elbow resting on the arm of her seat: Yvonne, my birth mother.

She saw me at the same time and shot up. Instinctively, I half-ran to her, and she hurried to meet me. My heart accelerated, my eyes misted. One, two, three, four steps and then we connected. We fell into each other's arms, both of us crying, tears of relief, tears of sadness, loss, tears of remembrance – tears of happiness, too, for the here and now.

I buried my face in her neck, wrapping my arms tight around her petite back, and cried and cried. Her skin felt so soft, and her smell … I recognised it, the scent of my birth mother, and I thought, *I've come home*.

Yvonne stroked my back as we hugged, it just felt so natural. I wanted to collapse in her arms – to really be held. In that moment I was a baby again. I remembered her. No words were spoken, no words were needed, our feelings instead communicated through touch and tears.

We stood there in the courtyard, locked in a tender embrace for minutes, both of us unable to let go. All the emotions I'd felt throughout childhood – the pain and rejection, the frustration and longing when I'd sat cross-legged in front of the bathroom mirror, trying to conjure an image of my birth mother – gushed out of me. Yvonne sobbed on my shoulder, letting her own emotions go too. We let it all out, oblivious to the people around us – this emotion needed to come, to have a voice at last.

I can't remember who spoke first, but we chatted away excitedly when we finally sat down, a few other guests casting us curious glances as we dabbed our eyes (Yvonne had come well-equipped with tissues). We didn't care. We were too caught up in the moment to notice anybody else. My body instinctively remembered Yvonne's voice as she put her hand beside mine on the table and said, 'Look, we even have the same hands.'

'I know,' I said, 'we have the same build. Small framed, little hands, slim fingers.'

We both gasped when we noticed that we were each wearing an identical ring – a gold 1950s' band, set with three small diamonds inside engraved stars.

'Ah, that was my mum's once,' Yvonne said, nodding at the ring finger on her right hand.

I smiled down at our hands, which were more or less the same size. 'Oh, that's so lovely, Yvonne. This ring belonged to my adoptive nan – Nanny Mac. What a coincidence.'

We hugged again at the table. 'I can't begin to tell you how wonderful it is to finally meet you in person, Liz. I was so nervous about today, but when I saw you, when I held you, I …'

Yvonne's eyes filled again. I couldn't stop looking at her – the tilt of her head, her blonde hair, shoulder-length like mine, her bottom lip trembling when she cried – I saw so much of myself in her. We'd even dressed in a similar way; Yvonne had on a white, sleeveless top, cotton like my red one, and a floral-print knee-length skirt.

'I was a nervous wreck too,' I said, fresh tears trickling down my face. 'I wasn't sure whether to hug you, but when I saw you, it just felt right.'

Yvonne smiled warmly. 'I was the same. I said to Martin, "How do I greet Liz? I don't know what to do." I'm glad that you did want to cuddle me though.'

As if on cue, we both looked up.

'Here comes Dan,' I said as he approached the table, carrying a tray of drinks. He was with another man.

'Here comes Martin,' said Yvonne, at exactly the same moment.

Dan set down the tray and motioned with his head at the man beside him. 'Look who I bumped into at the bar. Liz, meet Martin. We got chatting and I told him I was here with my wife, who's meeting her birth mother for the first time.'

Martin laughed. 'Then I said to him, "Well, that's a coincidence. My partner is meeting her daughter for the first time here today, too."'

We all laughed as we greeted each other, Martin giving me a warm squeeze and Dan enveloping Yvonne in one of his bear hugs. Then everyone settled down. Martin seemed lovely; he had grey eyes and was softly spoken, with a calming aura. After our emotional reunion, the mood felt relaxed. The four of us chatted for a bit – everyday conversations about holidays and such. We ordered food at some point, a lunch that I don't even remember eating. My recollections of that special day are entirely about Yvonne and me, getting to know one another, face to face, shoulder to shoulder in that sun-drenched courtyard.

Yvonne had brought some photos along, including one of me and her, captured by Mrs Roberts during my weeks in foster care. 'You can ask me anything, I don't mind,' said Yvonne as we studied the picture. There we were, in Mrs Roberts's lounge, Yvonne aged twenty, holding me. In this photo, Yvonne has beautiful, silky chestnut hair, tumbling over one shoulder as she beams at me, resting against her seventies-style brown-and-white polka-dot dress, my eyes squeezed shut, weeks-old mouth agape in a yawn. The expression on Yvonne's face is one of pure admiration, her smile iridescent in the light of the flashbulb. She looks like a happy young mum, bouncing her newborn on her knee. Our tragic story of the separation and heartache that awaited us is absent in this photograph.

The men left Yvonne and me to it; they chatted between themselves, made frequent trips to the bar, and even went for a walk so we could have time alone as mother and daughter. We moved onto the next two photographs, which Yvonne positioned side by side. The black-and-white picture on the left depicted Yvonne as a baby, nestled in a blanket, her fingers clenched in tiny fists at her chest. The second photograph, in colour, was of me as a baby, adopting a similar pose to Yvonne – a little balled left fist, my shock of auburn hair bright against the white pillow. The similarities between our features were striking in these two pictures. 'Look, we even have the same piggy nose,' I said, pointing at both pictures in turn.

'Yes, that's what I said to Martin: these could be pictures of one baby. We have the same shaped head, nose ... even the same amount of hair, although, I was dark, and you had that little mop of ginger hair.' Yvonne smiled into her shoulder. 'You know, I got a such a shock when I first saw your hair. I thought, *where's she got that from?*'

I giggled with Yvonne; it felt so good to be there with her. Our connection was instant, instinctive, and seeing the photographs prompted a question I'd been meaning to ask her for years. I lightly touched her forearm. 'Yvonne, there is something I'd like to ask you, if that's okay?'

'Of course. As I said, feel free to ask me anything.'

I lifted the foster home photograph, angling it as though it were displayed in a picture frame on the table. 'Why did you name me Claire? I've always cherished that you gave me a name. It felt like your little gift, to me.'

Yvonne paused for a moment. 'Well, I got that name from the Gilbert O'Sullivan song – it's called "Clair". It was a big hit in the early seventies. When I first heard it, I thought, *I really like the name and, one day, if I'm lucky enough to have a baby daughter, I'll call her Claire.* So, that's what I did – and I didn't want to let you go, I swear.'

I put my hand over Yvonne's on the table, it felt like a natural thing to do. 'I know. It must've been so painful for you. To have given me a name, knowing that you couldn't keep me. But the song … that's so special. I must listen to it.'

'Oh, and your middle name, Elaine,' said Yvonne, 'that's after a good friend who lived over the road from me when I was pregnant with you. She was ever so good to me, the only friend I had who knew about my pregnancy. I cried on Elaine's shoulder so many times.'

The afternoon melted away, rich with memories and reflections, revelations, laughter and tears.

Dan and Martin took photographs of Yvonne and me, on our compact film cameras. When we later got those pictures developed, I could see for myself the resemblance between us.

We had the same posture – both sitting with one elbow on the arms of our seats, leaning towards each other like bookends.

I discovered so much with Yvonne during our few hours at The Bear Hotel – more than could ever be expressed in letters and phone calls. The Yvonne I knew from the picture she'd sent in the post came to life before my eyes.

Now I could really visualise Yvonne as a nineteen-year-old pregnant woman, vulnerable and scared, hiding her bump beneath the 'boxy' maroon dress she described to me: 'It was a straight-up-and-down dress, but very roomy, so my tiny bump barely showed.' I imagined her crying on Elaine's shoulder, the heartbreak she must have felt whenever 'Clair' came on the radio. We talked again about the song that afternoon. 'I still find it difficult to listen to it,' Yvonne told me. 'I tried listening to that record a couple of times after they took you away from me. I'd get halfway through and then I'd have to turn it off – it just brought everything I'd been through, and everything I was now going through back to me.'

I asked Yvonne whether she'd had any cravings during her pregnancy, and she clapped her hands to her face, laughing. 'Junk food – burgers and fries,' she recalled. 'I couldn't get enough of them when I was pregnant.'

Certain smells and music also reminded Yvonne of her days carrying me. 'I wasn't keen on eggs,' she said, wrinkling her nose. 'The smell of them used to turn my stomach.

'We'd hear a lot of songs by The Monkees and David Essex on the radio back then, but one song that sticks in my mind from my days carrying you was that Christmas song by Slade. That was played *everywhere* – in shops, on the radio, the telly. You'd kick like mad to that song.'

'Oh gosh, Yvonne, that's "Merry Xmas Everybody" – it was still number one when you gave birth to me. I then recalled how I'd shivered when I'd heard it in the shop at Charing Cross Station in 1997. 'As soon as it started playing, something shifted inside of me. I imagined an invisible cord, connecting us, stretching way up into the sky. That's when I contacted Jenny – I knew the moment had come to contact you.'

Yvonne put her arm over my shoulders. 'I'm so glad that you did, Liz.'

We were joining the dots, enriching the paintings of our pasts, exposing our wounds, and I appreciated Yvonne's openness. Her biggest revelation, however, was yet to come …

Just before we said our farewells, after Martin and Yvonne insisted paying for our lunch – 'You're my daughter – and Martin has gained a stepdaughter – we're paying for this and that's final' – Yvonne retrieved a yellow Post-it note from her handbag. 'Now, I don't know how you feel about this, Liz, but the other day, Andy, your birth father, called me.'

'Really?' I was taken aback. I'd often thought about Andy, but hadn't yet considered finding him – Yvonne had always been the parent at the forefront of my mind, that everlasting yearning for my mother. 'How did he find you?'

'He got my number from the phonebook. I didn't recognise his voice after all these years. I said, "Andy who?" when I picked up the phone. Anyway, I hope you don't mind, but I told him that you and I were now in touch, and he said he'd love to meet you too, but he doesn't want to upset the apple cart – those were his words. He said it's entirely up to you.' Yvonne handed me the Post-it note. 'On there is Andy's email address. I promised him I'd forward it to you, just in case you'd like to contact him.'

'Thank you, Yvonne, this is incredible,' I said, staring at my birth father's address. 'And yes, I think I would like to contact him at some point.'

'Well, he said he'll send me some photographs – he has other children too. He mentioned a daughter, but I can't remember who else. I can forward the pictures to you if you like?'

'So, I've got a half-sister?' This was a shock, albeit a comforting one – I'd always wanted a sister.

Yvonne nodded. 'Let's just say it seems Andy's been very busy on the children front over the years.'

We left the courtyard then, but as we entered the archway that led into the hotel, I glanced over my shoulder, at our vacant table, a reminder that today really had happened, Yvonne and my shared DNA lingering on our empty glasses. The parasol shivered, caught by a sudden breeze – or maybe it was moved, trembling at the scenes it had observed over the last few hours. I said a silent goodbye to our courtyard of memories, to the day that I first met my birth mother.

Our farewell in the car park was as emotional as our earlier greeting. Yvonne and I collapsed into each other's arms, both crying. 'My daughter,' Yvonne sobbed. 'I'll treasure this day forever.'

'Me too,' I whispered, and breathed in her scent again. *I've come home.*

We said our goodbyes, then left in our respective cars. Dan and I headed one way, Yvonne and Martin in the opposite direction.

'Well, that went well,' said Dan.

'Yes, it did,' I replied. 'Thank you for arranging today, darling – it meant everything to me.' I still felt overwhelmed, and a little strange. After our unstoppable outpourings of emotions, Yvonne and I were returning to our everyday lives. On the drive back to Surrey, I relived my meeting with Yvonne in my head, remembering who had said what and when, our touches, her smell. I thought about Andy and my half-siblings, and whether I wanted to find them. *Where should I start?*

The following morning, while Dan was at football training, I went online to look for the Gilbert O'Sullivan song that Yvonne had mentioned. I was intrigued to listen to the track and discover its meaning.

I found the song – I think I bought it on iTunes – and pressed play. I leaned back in my wicker chair in front of the computer and closed my eyes. It was a beautiful, gentle song, beginning with Gilbert O'Sullivan whistling a lilting melody before singing the first word: 'Clair'. The lyrics were so poignant.

In the piece, O'Sullivan sings about the moment he first met 'Clair', describing a deep connection he felt with her, but somehow, he can't explain this wonderous feeling. He can't put it into words, he sings.

I cried during the chorus, when O'Sullivan pours his heart out, still trying to convey his love for Clair, and the special moments spent with her that he'll never forget, and I thought, *I'm named after this song, but who's O'Sullivan's Clair?*

My heart pulsed to the steady 4/4 time signature, strummed on the guitar. O'Sullivan mentioned 'Uncle Ray', and the song ended with the echo of a little girl's laughter.

Next, I returned to the keyboard and typed, 'Meaning of the song "Clair" by Gilbert O'Sullivan' into Google. This led me to an informative article, which explained the artist's inspiration for the song.

'Clair' was the young daughter of his manager, whom O'Sullivan was staying with when he wrote the song. In interviews, O'Sullivan has told how he'd hear little Clair's cries from the next room during the night. He was going through a tough time dealing with his parents' separation at the time, so he'd distract himself by playing with Clair, who called him 'Uncle Ray'. They formed a strong, 'unforgettable' bond.

So, Clair was a little girl. I listened to the song again, now understanding its meaning, and my thoughts instantly turned to Yvonne and me during my first eight weeks. How must I have felt, waking up in the night in the nursery, crying for my mother, who was under the same hospital roof but banned from comforting me? I imagined myself, as a baby, crying for Yvonne in the foster home, and when I was taken from her arms for the final time.

The parallels between the song and our story struck me. *No wonder Yvonne finds it hard to listen to this. It must've played in her head continuously throughout those eight weeks and beyond.*

I wiped my eyes and opened my A4 notebook. I wanted to write to Yvonne, to thank her for our lunch the previous day. To thank her for the special moment that, like O'Sullivan, I would never forget. I wrote this letter for me, and for Yvonne, and for Claire, whom we'll both never forget.

11

I've Missed Out on So Much

Later that week, I received a letter, closely followed by a parcel, from Yvonne.

In her letter, a reply to my last one, she wrote about our reunion and the hot weather we'd been having lately. I curled up on the sofa to read her latest instalment, feeling a new-found closeness to my birth mother since we'd met. I giggled in places – Yvonne was so entertaining in her notes. But I was upset to read that she'd suffered another accident:

Dear Liz,

We too had a wonderful time last Friday. It was so lovely to finally meet you face to face – and to meet Dan, too. Me and Martin were only just saying what a lovely young man he [Dan] is. I'm so happy that you're being looked after by him, Liz – he clearly idolises you.

I can't begin to tell you how special our meeting was. It really did mean the world to me – I'll cherish that day in my heart until my dying day. I haven't stopped thinking – or talking – about it.

We wouldn't have expected you to pay for your lunch, so you're both more than welcome. Martin didn't tell me until today, but when he'd gone walkabout with Dan, they came across a fish-and-chip shop, so Martin had some chips. Sneaky little devil – he kept that one quiet, didn't he. I called him a little piggy as he also had a curry on Friday evening – I only had some chips.

It has been very warm again. Most unpleasant having to work in that heat. As soon as I get home from work, I strip off and put shorts and a bikini top on – the least clothes the better.

Poor cats just don't know where to go to be in the cool. I've even been putting ice cubes in their water.

I had a little accident on Sunday. I decided to have a quick shower before we went to a BBQ. When I'd finished, as I went to step out of the shower, my left foot slipped, and I caught all the inside of my right leg and banged my head on the basin. It bruised straight away, and it looks rather horrible at the moment, but I'm getting better, day by day.

I will ring you on Thursday at 7 o'clock. Hope that's okay with you.

Well, I had better get the tea ready. Enjoy the weekend and I look forward to speaking to you soon.

All our love,

From

Yvonne & Martin

xx

I too hadn't stopped thinking about my reunion with Yvonne. For all our prior nerves and fears, we couldn't have wished for a more magical day.

Yvonne's parcel arrived two days after her letter, on a Saturday morning. I read her accompanying note first:

Dear Liz,

Just a little note with this little gift.

Martin and I went for one of our walks yesterday. We were looking for a present for my neighbour Margaret, who was feeding the cats. Anyway, while I was in the shop, I came across this, and it took my eye. After reading the words, I thought that it was very appropriate. Hope you don't mind.

I've also enclosed the photos of Andy, which arrived this morning. Andy doesn't seem to have changed much to me, apart from perhaps being a little thicker set.

Speak to you soon.

Love from

Yvonne

x

I tipped the contents of the Jiffy bag onto my lap: an envelope and a tissue-wrapped present. Inside the envelope were two photographs. One picture captured Andy with a baby boy, who I assumed must be his son. I saw a smiling man in his late forties, with thickish short dark hair, lightly threaded with grey at the sides. He was wearing a T-shirt and sitting on a sofa, cradling a cuddly toy in one arm and the boy in the other. Andy had a square chin, like mine, and I could see a similarity between us around the nose. His eyes were a greenish blue, like mine, but a slightly lighter shade. Deep, soulful eyes, I thought.

The second photo showed Andy in a baseball cap, again holding a little boy, but I couldn't decide whether this was the same child as in the first picture.

It was hard to comprehend that I was staring at my birth father. The emotional tug felt different from when I'd first seen Yvonne's photographs. She had known me for eight weeks, but

Andy hadn't even seen me as a baby. I hadn't bonded with him like I had with my birth mother.

Looking at those pictures of Andy brought a mixture of emotions to the surface – sadness for our mutual loss, the missing years; sorrow for him – according to my adoption papers he'd expressed a wish to 'bring me up' with his fiancée. *Had he also looked for me like Yvonne had done, and grieved for what could have been? What happened that day at the Barratt Maternity Home, when my 'putative' father was turned away by staff. Did he put up a fight? Could he fill in the gaps regarding his relationship with Yvonne – the parts she couldn't remember?* My mind went into overdrive again with questions about my past, but mostly, I was curious to know more about Andy. *What kind of life had he led? Who is this stranger smiling in these glossy photographs? And who is my half-sister?* Feeling comfortable after my successful reunion with Yvonne, I felt confident and ready to meet Andy, to find out more about the man who was denied the opportunity to see his newborn daughter.

I put the photographs to one side and picked up Yvonne's gift. *How thoughtful of her.* Beneath the lilac tissue paper was a wooden, heart-shaped plaque bearing the message, *A daughter is someone you love with all your heart.* This choked and confused me at once. I was touched by Yvonne's sweet gesture, but I also realised, *My adoptive mother, the person I know as 'Mum', has never bought me a sentimental ornament like this.*

I hadn't yet told Mum and Dad about my meeting with Yvonne. I didn't want to navigate their reactions, or their questions, and besides, our reunion was about us, Yvonne and me. It was *our* story, *our* choice.

Yvonne's gift spoke volumes; she always sent heartfelt cards on my birthday and at Christmas – she'd sent Dan and me a lovely first anniversary card, with the greeting, *To a very special daughter and son-in-law.* Her cards always had 'daughter' written on the front, with poignant verses inside. She'd write touching, personal messages, too.

I remember Mum and Dad visiting us to celebrate my birthday one year. My cards were displayed on the mantelpiece in our lounge, including one from Yvonne, emblazoned with 'To my lovely daughter' and another 'daughter' card from Mum. 'Let's have a look at your cards then, Elizabeth,' she said.

'I've got some lovely ones this year,' I replied.

Of course, she made a beeline for Yvonne's greeting. I saw the thunder rumble across her face as she opened it and read the words penned inside.

She then put it back on the mantelpiece, tucked behind another card, tutting to herself.

I got up from the sofa then, walked purposefully over to the mantelpiece and put Yvonne's card back in its rightful place. 'These are *mine*, and they're *all* special to me.'

She shot one last disdainful look at it, making a noise of contempt under her breath.

I sat for a while, gazing at Yvonne's gift, at the word 'daughter', and sighed. *When will I have a daughter – or a son?* Dan and I had been trying for a baby for several months now. Fortunately, the chemotherapy hadn't affected his fertility, but he still had to go for regular sperm analysis tests.

Our trying for a baby had become more of a mission than a series of romantic interludes. We were doing everything by the book. I kept a chart, monitoring my ovulation dates, ensured I ate healthily to maintain a good weight. I cut out alcohol, avoided excessive exercise, read all the 'trying for a baby' books, but still, I hadn't become pregnant.

We'd visited our GP, who said it could take time for this to happen. 'We usually recommend waiting between two and five years after chemotherapy before trying for a child,' he'd said, then went on to remind us about Dan's banked sperm. 'It's useable for up to ten years, so you still have that option, but hopefully, you'll fall pregnant.'

Our doctor had a point, but we desperately wanted things to happen naturally.

What if I never fall pregnant? I shook my head as though to physically eradicate that grievous thought and looked again at my pictures of Andy, searching for fragments of me in his features. *What does he do for a living? How many half-siblings do I have? I will email Andy,* I decided. *I'll do it right now.*

I sat down at our computer, typed a sentence, deleted it, typed another sentence and erased that too. I did this a few times until I found the right words to say to my birth father. I began:

Dear Andy,
Hope you're well.

Yvonne kindly gave me your email address, so I thought I'd write to you. I must admit, this does feel strange. You're my biological father, yet we've never met. However, I would like to get to know you as I've always been curious about my beginnings.

I see from the photographs that Yvonne sent you that we're alike in some ways – we have the same square jawline, similar noses.

I paused to attach a photograph, so Andy could see what I looked like, choosing one that Dan took of me on a recent visit to Wisley Gardens Manor House, Surrey. I'm smiling into the sunshine in this picture, casual in a hooded tracksuit top, the stately house sprawling on the horizon behind me.

Then I told Andy a little about myself and Dan – our jobs, where we lived. I asked him about his life, too, before moving on to more serious questions about him and Yvonne:

> I have many questions to ask you about how you and Yvonne met – where did you first meet? How long were you together for? Why were you 'forbidden' from seeing either of us in the hospital – and by whom?
>
> So, that was it – after Yvonne found out she was pregnant, you had no further contact with Yvonne or me again? What did that feel like?
>
> It also says in the extensive paperwork records I have from The Children's Society that you were engaged to another woman for some time and that you had even offered to 'take me on'. It even uses the word 'putative' when it talks about you being the father – I wonder why that was?
>
> I still have so many questions about what happened back then – sorry to fire them all at you, but it will help me put together my beginnings, and I want to get your side of the story too.
>
> If you want to ask me any questions, I'm also fine with that.

I signed off and pressed 'send', hoping I hadn't bombarded Andy with too much information too soon.

Andy's reply landed in my inbox the following evening. It was an extensive reply in which he divulged some harrowing details of his life growing up. I found his writing beautiful – sensitive, intelligent and honest – and, like Yvonne, he seemed good humoured.

It felt a bit surreal. As I read Andy's many paragraphs, I had to keep reminding myself, *This is my birth father, speaking to me for the first time.* I wondered what he sounded like, although I did get a feel for his voice in his email titled 'The Origin of Species':

Dear Liz,

Things have moved on somewhat since Darwin's time, but with so much water having flowed under the bridge, knowing how, or even where to begin is no easy task. I guess you started the ball rolling by going in search of your 'biological roots'. I can empathise with your decision to do so. When I was 27, I finally summoned the courage to search for my 'dad'.

My parents divorced when I was six, as a result of my dad's violent behaviour towards my mum – due to his excessively heavy drinking. To cut a long story short, he had nothing to do with my mum or me since the divorce. He remarried, emigrated to New Zealand, and had two more sons (apparently, though I've never had any contact). Unfortunately, I left it too late to go searching, as he had committed suicide some four years earlier. This event left a lasting impression on me. For years I wrestled with the knowledge of your existence, and the possibility that you might search for your genetic parents one day.

I can imagine how you're keen to 'put some flesh' on the missing parts of your 'beginnings'. As you may have gathered, although I have always been an 'absent' parent, I can honestly say that you have never been absent from my thoughts. I understand that still leaves a huge void of unanswered questions, and I shall attempt to answer as many of them as I can, but (yes, unfortunately there is a 'but') …

I re-read the above paragraphs, identifying the prominent themes running through my biological family – loss, abandonment, violence, rejection, grief, and trauma. I wondered how much of his childhood Andy remembered. He must have witnessed those violent episodes at home as a young boy – how could he even begin to process such agony?

Sadness engulfed me when he wrote about 'wrestling' with knowledge of my existence. I thought about him, thinking about me, wondering where I was and what I was doing for twenty-nine lost years. It was mind-boggling, incomprehensible almost. *I've never been absent from his thoughts.*

However, Andy did shed some light on his relationship with Yvonne:

I left the navy in 1973 and met Yvonne (who lived 'down the road' at the time). We were young and carefree and had a whirlwind romance that lasted a few months. Yvonne became pregnant and our parents stepped in to seize control of the situation. When you were born (yes, you're my eldest as it happens) I was 'forbidden' from visiting you in the hospital and instructed to stay away from Yvonne thereafter – because (I was told) she didn't want to see me ever again. The rest is history, and I really never expected to see or hear from Yvonne ever again. Time is a healer, I guess. Subsequently, I went through a bewildering period of highly confusing relationships, usually, ironically, involving women with children.

I sense Yvonne still carries an enormous burden in respect of what happened then – and since – and possibly because you are her 'only' child, she may be experiencing an intensity of challenging emotions, as she not only comes to terms with the present and future of our rediscovered relationships, but also as she relives those anguishing moments of so long ago.

What wicked lengths Andy's mum and Yvonne's dad went to. Reading Andy's account, I remembered Yvonne once telling me how she'd desperately tried to contact Andy when I was in the foster home. 'I tried calling him,' she told me, 'but his mother would always hang up or say, "No, he's not here – and he doesn't want anything to do with you." One day, I even went up to the fire station where he worked, but the bosses wouldn't let me in – or let Andy out.' And lost amid that storm of collusion, control and contempt was an innocent baby – me. I had a name, but I didn't have a voice – and neither did Yvonne or Andy.

I learned a lot about my birth father in that one email. Andy lived in Wales with his wife, Rebecca. They were renovating their home – a former derelict farmhouse, he said.

Andy described himself as 'fairly creative', 'resourceful' and 'very practical'. Although a 'reluctant scholar', he had a postgraduate diploma in countryside management and worked part-time in environmental conservation.

Around his outdoors job, he also worked as a support worker, helping people with mental health issues and learning difficulties. Coincidentally, he also studied complementary therapy, massage and aromatherapy, like me. Already, a common thread connected us. Andy struck me as being very much in tune with his emotions, too:

Thank you for sending that photo of you. It really does capture your true beauty (despite the chimneys on top of your head). I know it sounds daft, but I've looked at it frequently throughout the day, and experienced a whole range of overwhelming feelings and emotions. Mostly, these have made me smile happily, but at times I've wept tears of joy (I'm a big softy).

When I married Rebecca, I decided to tell her about you, so that if anything were to happen to me in the meantime, she would be able to act as a link between you and your genetic 'siblings', should you decide to go searching (and for some reason, I thought you just might).

After twenty-nine years there is a great deal to take on board for all concerned. I recently found myself having a conversation with Yvonne, who I never expected to meet, ever again. Now suddenly, you and I are faced with the prospect of perhaps opening a new chapter in our lives. Mine comes with a lot of 'baggage'. It's a fairly big can of worms, but if you want to open it, rest assured, I'll be here, ready and waiting. Whatever you decide, whenever, at least you know the door will always be open to you.

I have added my phone number below, although I understand if you don't want to speak yet. Certainly, emotions are easier to handle like this. Hope to hear from you soon.

Much love,

Andy

I replied to Andy's message, thanking him for recounting his search for his father, which had assured me that he was 'more than equipped to understand my situation'.

My fingers pitter-pattered over the keys – I had so much more to ask Andy, especially about my half-siblings. I was so curious to know who these strangers who shared my genes were. *Do they look like me?*

Finally, the genetic mirroring I'd longed for growing up was happening. I could now say things such as, 'I get my musical and creative talents from my birth mother.' Or, 'I've got Yvonne's hands and slight frame.' If people were to ask me where my love for aromatherapy and complementary therapy came from, I could proudly answer, 'My birth father – he's a qualified therapist too.'

Questions flowed in my responses to Andy.

I was flabbergasted to hear that you're trained in aromatherapy and massage – so am I. Quite unbelievable and what a coincidence! How and when did you do that? What are you doing these days? Can you tell me more about your support work? It sounds fascinating.

It also makes me feel nice that you say you wrestled with my existence (hopefully in a positive way) as I was always curious to know whether you and Yvonne were thinking about me, wondering what I was doing – and whether you wanted to be 'found'.

How many half-sisters and brothers do I have? It's difficult for me to keep track. So, I'm your eldest, then? Do your other children know about me? If so, how did they react?

My goodness, so many questions. It's difficult to know where to start, isn't it – for both of us to fill each other in, but I think it's really exciting.

Lastly, Andy, I want to thank you for being so willing and open to contact and questions, and for being so positive about speaking with Yvonne, too. I appreciate that it can't be easy for either of you after all these years. It was always a worry – how exactly I would pursue you both independently, but it has worked out so well and you are both being so positive, so, thank you.

Sorry if this email has been a bit of a babble – there are so many things I want to discover. It's difficult to know where to start and not to go round and round in circles.

Looking back, I realise I was in the 'honeymoon' phase of my reunion process. I was excited, emboldened; my contact with Andy moved rapidly – and I felt surprisingly comfortable with this. After a few more emails back and forth, we arranged a telephone call. I couldn't wait to hear his voice.

I called Andy one evening after work. 'Hi Andy, it's just me,' I said casually, as if I'd known him all my life.

'It's so good to hear your voice, Liz. I can't begin to tell you how delighted I am to be in contact with you at last.' His voice was soft, expressive, with a very slight lilting accent and loaded with gentleness. The voice of my birth father soothed me. His tone captivated me like a child being read a story book, its eloquence and reassurance drew me in each time we spoke. 'I'm so sorry, for the past … the way things turned out.'

'It's lovely to hear you, too. You sound just like how you write in your emails, Andy. How are you?'

'Well, we're a bit upside down just now with these house renovations. We'll be glad when things get back to normal. But tell me about you, Liz. How're *you* feeling?'

We chatted for a while about aromatherapy, my adoption and when I first searched for Yvonne and our subsequent reunion many years later. Andy was easy to talk to. He was a good listener, I felt that he was genuinely interested in me.

'So, do you mind me asking, Andy,' I said, as the conversation shifted to family life, 'about my half-siblings. I've been so curious. How many do I have?'

Andy paused, cleared his throat. 'Are you sitting down, Liz?'

I laughed. 'Yes, I'm just on the sofa with my feet up – Dan's cooking tonight.'

'Well, you're the eldest of six.'

I nearly spilled my mug of tea. 'Six? Really? I know I have a sister, but who are the others?'

'So, there's …' Andy began, and proceeded to list the names of my half-brothers and sisters from various relationships. And this is where things become confusing.

After Yvonne gave birth to me, Andy went on to have a daughter, followed by a son, in 1976 and 1979 respectively, with his first wife of four years. 'Sadly, things didn't work out,' Andy explained. After moving to North Wales in 1982, Andy met his second wife, with whom he had a daughter Elinor, but they split up after six years. 'I have been in close contact with

Elinor throughout,' he added. He went on to have two sons with his third partner. 'We didn't plan to have children, but at thirty-five, her biological clock began to tick away, and she decided she would like to start a family of our own.'

'Gosh, Andy,' I said, 'I've always wanted a sister – now I have two. And three half-brothers. That's incredible.'

Elinor and my other half-sister in Australia knew about me and would be keen to get to know their 'big sister', should I wish, Andy told me. 'They've been asking all about you, Liz.'

'Yes, I'd like that – I'm fascinated to know what they look like.'

Andy laughed. 'Well, I think Elinor looks a lot like you. There are many similarities there.'

'Wow,' I said slowly, 'just, wow.' I had no other words.

* * *

I built up quite a rapport with Andy over the ensuing weeks. His messages were sincere, signed always 'with love'. Yvonne was happy that Andy and I were establishing a relationship, too.

In mid-October 2003, I thought about meeting Andy. Dan and I had planned a mini-break to Wales, so the timing was perfect.

I called Andy. 'How do you feel about meeting up?' I asked. 'We're coming to Wales at the end of the month.'

'Oh, Liz, of course, I'd love to see you,' he said. 'Would you like to meet Elinor too?'

'Absolutely, I've been thinking so much about my half-sisters and brothers.'

We arranged to meet for lunch on 27 October, a Monday.

I didn't feel the same nervousness about meeting Andy and Elinor as I'd had before my reunion with Yvonne. This time, my stomach fluttered with excitable apprehension – and deep, yearning curiosity.

As we pulled up outside The Lamb and Flag Inn, a cosy bar nestled in the heart of the beautiful market town, Rhayader, I told Dan, 'I have a good feeling about today.'

'I think that's them, over there.' I followed his gaze left to the approaching man with pewter-coloured hair, a teenage girl alongside him.

'Yes, that's *him*,' I said, 'that's Andy – and Elinor. Gosh, I can see already how she looks like me. Look, darling.'

I unclipped my seatbelt, stepped out of the car and hurried across the car park, towards the man with outstretched arms. 'Andy,' I cried.

'Well, hello, Liz.'

'It's so lovely to meet you,' were my first words, as I wrapped my arms around my birth father. It felt so natural, just as it had when I'd first hugged Yvonne.

'I can't believe it,' said Andy, holding me tight. 'After all these years. This is so exciting.'

I greeted Elinor next while Andy and Dan shook hands. 'My little sister,' I said as we hugged.

'And you're my big sister.' Her voice carried a tone of familiarity, and she really did look the image of me.

It's difficult for me to recall the exact conversations we had over lunch, but I do remember Andy's poignant words when we talked about our missing years, his eyes glistening with hurt behind tinted glasses.

He looked me in the eye from his seat across the table. 'I wasn't even allowed to see you at the hospital, Liz. We were both denied that opportunity. There was a huge chunk of your life when you couldn't have a relationship with your birth parents and …' His voice cracked. He closed his eyes for a few seconds, 'it devastates me that you were also denied that. You were *always* in my thoughts.'

I welled up too. 'It was difficult … for all of us, but I'm glad we three have reconnected.' I smiled at Elinor. 'And I'm thrilled to have gained little sisters and brothers.'

'We're here for you, whenever you need, Liz.'

I tilted my head, in the same manner I remembered Yvonne had done the first time I'd met her in person. 'I know. Thank you, Andy.'

I couldn't stop looking at Andy and Elinor, at their faces, their eyes, my genes. Visually, there was so much to take in. I was fascinated, watching their movements, and comparing their features to mine.

Every time I glanced at Andy, I caught him looking at me, too. It was almost as though my nervous system was trying to read him, to capture everything, drink in his mannerisms and note the inflections in his voice. I searched for quirks, gestures that prompted me to think, *Oh, look, that's me.* My adoptive mother had always warned me, *It's rude to stare, Elizabeth*, but on this occasion, I couldn't help it, and neither could Andy. This was my flesh and blood, my history and reality, animated before me.

'Sorry, I was just looking at your eyes,' I said to Andy at one point. 'They're so green – just like Elinor's and similar to mine.'

Andy smiled. 'I was just thinking the same thing.'

Elinor, petite with blonde shoulder-length hair, had the same smile as me. She seemed quite nervous, but we talked about her interests. 'I'm sitting my GCSEs in the summer,' she told me.

Andy spoke about his children, including my other sister Natalie, who lived in Australia. 'She's thrilled to have a big sister – she's asked for your email address, but I said I'd check with you, first, Liz.'

'Yes, of course,' I said. I was still stunned to discover I had so many half-siblings.

It was twilight when we parted company, in the car park of the Lamb and Flag, an earthy smell of autumn in the air. I hugged Elinor, then Andy, goodbye. 'I hope we haven't scared you off,' he said.

'I hope you don't think I was rude … staring at you both so much.'

We let go and looked at each other in the dusky light. Silent for a few seconds, both mourning the loss of twenty-nine years. 'I'm sorry,' said Andy, 'for what happened all those years ago. But I want you to know that the door is always open, Liz. You'll never be alone.'

I hugged him again. 'It was lovely to meet you, to see you. Goodbye, Andy. Take care.' As we parted, we both turned, glancing over our shoulders for one more look as we reached our respective cars.

The grief hit me as we drove away. While I was happy to have met Andy and Elinor, and to have heard about my half-siblings, I was struck with this new level of cognisance of all the time we had lost, the overwhelming possibilities of what could have been. My little sisters and brothers had all grown up knowing Andy, but I'd missed out. The tears came first, cutting slow, cold paths down my face. I turned my head and tried to hide the noise. I couldn't. I was sobbing now.

Dan's warm hand landed softly on my thigh. 'Bless you, darling – this must be so hard for you.'

I turned to face him, my eyes overflowing. 'I've missed out on so much.'

12

Spoken

South Road, Englefield Green, April 2004
I paced back and forth on the landing, trying to muster the courage to go back into the bathroom, fearing another unbearable disappointment.

My fingers were crossed on both hands as I held my stomach. *Please, please, please let it have worked this time.*

Resting on the edge of the sink behind the bathroom door was a white plastic wand – my latest pregnancy test, which I'd taken over ten minutes ago.

Dan and I had been trying for a baby for over a year now. I'd lost count of the number of times I'd sat on the edge of the bath, sobbing at yet another 'not pregnant' result, that single blue line, bold and hurtful in the window of the wand.

I took a deep breath and pushed open the bathroom door, reassuring myself, as always, *If it hasn't been successful this time, we could still use Dan's frozen sperm he had banked before his chemotherapy.* The wand was still where I'd left it, window-side down on the sink. Sitting in my usual spot, I reached for the test, holding it in my lap for a moment, eyes scrunched shut. *Please, please, please.* I opened my eyes, expecting the worst, but I blinked rapidly, my gasp echoing around the bathroom as I saw the two blue horizontal lines, bold and proud in the window. I checked again, to make absolutely sure. 'I'm pregnant,' I said to the sink. 'I'm pregnant,' I said to the bath, then I stood up, legs shaking, and looked into the bathroom mirror, at my teary smile. 'We're pregnant,' I whispered. 'We're actually pregnant.'

I couldn't believe our luck; I was over the moon! My first instinct was to call Dan at work, to tell him our happy news, but then I had an idea, *No, I'll surprise him this evening.*

It was a Monday morning, and I had the day off work. Hours stretched ahead before Dan was due home, and I was already feeling like I could burst with excitement. I wondered how on earth I'd be able to keep this to myself until he walked through the door.

I showered and dressed, working out the timescale of events in my head. *Our baby will arrive in December.* I'd read somewhere that at six weeks pregnant, your baby is the size of a fivepence.

For all the heartache we'd been through with Dan's cancer, then fearing we might never have children, my lifelong yearning for my own child and difficulties with my parents, my falling pregnant was so very important to us. This was our dream come true, and my dream since childhood. I couldn't help but wonder, *Will we have a girl? Will I finally get my baby Grace?*

I stepped out of the front door, beaming, and headed into Egham town centre. The little church on the high street was home to all manner of mother and baby groups and antenatal classes. Only a few months beforehand, I'd left a coffee shop, another popular place in town for new mums, in tears. It was sometimes too painful for me, being surrounded by babies with their mothers, watching the love and tenderness between them. Today was different.

Still smiling, I entered the card shop and went directly to the 'new baby' section. I studied each card carefully in turn, admiring their illustrations and verses, avoiding the 'It's a boy' and 'It's a girl' ones. Dan and I had previously decided that, if we did get pregnant, we wouldn't want to know the sex of our baby before the birth – the element of surprise added to the magic of the experience of being pregnant and, of course, the birth itself.

I wanted this card to be perfect. I found just the right card, by the talented photographer Anne Geddes, depicting a sleeping newborn baby on top of a cushion of fluffy folded towels. The photo was black and white, except for a corsage of two roses – one pink, the other cream, pinned to the base of the towelling pile. The message inside the card read, *Congratulations on the birth of your baby!*

As usual, the coffee shop was busy with mums and their babies. I ordered a drink and sat down, happy to observe for a while, catching snippets of conversations among the group of women at the next table, each interacting with their babies in different ways – some cooing, some bouncing their babies on their knees, smiling and laughing. 'She'll be fifteen weeks on Thursday,' I heard one mum say. I felt like shouting out to them, 'I'm pregnant!' but I didn't. Instead, I placed the card I'd just bought on the table and grabbed my pen, purse and a small reel of Sellotape out of my handbag. What the coffee shop symbolised had completely changed for me; it now felt like the perfect place to sit and write my card to Dan.

First, I took out a fivepence coin from my purse, which I taped just underneath the words inside. Then I got to work on tweaking that printed message. I crossed out 'birth', replacing it with 'conception', and omitted the y in 'your', so the new greeting read, 'Congratulations on the Conception of our Baby'. Beneath this, I wrote, 'Who is this big,' and drew an arrow pointing at the fivepence, 'And 6 weeks old! Due to meet us both in December 2004. All my love, Mummykins x'.

I sealed the card, feeling pleased with myself. *We're pregnant – and I can't wait to tell Dan, to see his reaction.* Sipping my coffee, I carried on watching the mums and babies. *Soon, I'll be part of your world too.*

I was perched on the stairs, ready to pounce when Dan came home from work. As soon as I heard his key enter the lock, I got up. 'What are you so happy about this evening?' he said as he came through the door. I hadn't stopped smiling all day.

'Here, this is for you.' I handed the card to Dan, who gave me a confused look.

'Have I forgotten an occasion? It's not our anniversary.'

'Open it.'

Dan pulled back his head in surprise as he tore open the envelope to reveal the Anne Geddes image.

'Look inside,' I urged.

I watched, unblinking, as he read my words; I didn't want to miss one expression on his face throughout this special moment. He looked at the card for a long time, taking in what I had written. His chest heaved, the card trembling in his hand, then he looked at me, tears pooling in his eyes.

'You're *pregnant*? We're going to have a *baby*?'

'Yes! I did a test this morning. Our baby is the size of a fivepence piece. I've been *dying* to tell you all day!' I hugged him and we stood in the hallway, holding onto each other, crying tears of joy.

'We did it,' Dan smiled through his tears.

We were deliriously happy, and I absolutely loved being pregnant. I read all the books and kept a diary, charting my pregnancy at every stage. We worked out that our baby would arrive on 1 December, which was confirmed at my three-month scan.

I felt so protective of this little person, growing inside of me. We shared our news with friends and family after my first scan. My adoptive parents were happy for us. Yvonne was over the moon when I told her. 'Oh, I'm going to be a grandmother,' she gushed down the phone.

Yvonne, Andy and I kept in touch via writing and phone calls, but I was still processing my thoughts and emotions in the wake of seeing them both. Andy sent me a lovely email after our meeting in Wales:

Subject: Us

Dear Liz,

It was absolutely wonderful to meet up with you and Dan. You were both very 'comfortable' to be with, in what was, when all said and done, a fairly unusual situation.

Twenty-nine years is a long time to wait to hold your first-born child in your arms, and to look into her eyes for the very first time. I simply cannot put into words how important our meeting was to me.

I hope you will forgive me for not being 'there' throughout your life. That's a lot to ask, I know, but I also realise that you have experienced a kind of upbringing that I could never have provided.

Dan is a great guy too – a real 'gentle giant'. I can see why you are so attracted to him (not that I am, I hasten to add … even if we did play footsie under the table!).

I'm really glad that Elinor was with us. She was very nervous, as I'm sure you would have realised, but you put her at ease, and she was really happy to have met you. It seems to have inspired a hope that she'll share your progression to beauty as she 'matures' (the vain rationality of a sixteen-year-old or what!)

It's reassuring to find that you are such a warm, open and tactile person. I can appreciate how difficult this 'journey' must have been. I'm sure that, over the years, you must have wrestled with a whole gamut of emotions, encompassing just about everything possible as you tried to come to terms with the whys and wherefores of what happened. I'm really glad you stuck with it, Liz. It seems so inadequate to plead 'immaturity', but to be honest, in hindsight, that was what it was. I'm still not sure when one is deemed to have 'grown up', if indeed one ever does grow up. I guess it's really a matter of accepting responsibility – and I'm ready for that.

After our meeting, I phoned Yvonne to ease her natural curiosity. She asked how things had gone between us and what we had discussed. I think that she may have wanted to organise things a little differently, with perhaps her being a little more involved. However, we seem to have progressed somewhat 'organically' at our own pace, and I make no apology for that. She seems genuinely happy that we (you and I) have been able to establish contact, but she appears to have her own slant on the relationship that exists between you.

Having six children doesn't 'dilute' the way you feel about any of them. In fact, speaking from experience, I can say that you have to tread quite carefully in certain circumstances in order to not put anyone's noses out of joint. However, in Yvonne's case you are everything to her, which can be a little daunting, I'm sure. I'm happy to re-establish contact with her after all this time. I get the impression we are quite different, but at the end of the day, we are (for all our faults) still your 'flesh and blood' (poor you).

Meanwhile, thanks to you and Dan. I'm sure you'll want to reflect on our meeting. I guess that I've finally had the chance to chill out and reflect on the magic of our day. Bizarre indeed, but wonderful, nonetheless.

You know where we are and, to some extent, who we are. I hope you choose to take us on board.

Bye for now.

With love,

Andy XX

Andy had fully acknowledged the pain I'd suffered, that I still 'wrestled with a whole gamut of emotions' relating to my beginnings.

When I'd met Yvonne and Andy I was in a celebratory headspace, swept away in the magic of my discoveries. After years of wondering who my birth parents were, and what they looked like, I'd finally found them – and they wanted me to be a part of their lives. I'd been so excited to discover I had five half-siblings, especially two younger sisters, but the immensity and reality of what I'd missed out on, what could've been, had hit me hard after I'd said goodbye to Andy in the car park of The Lamb and Flag Inn.

Adoption reunions, as I was discovering, are complicated, emotionally challenging and difficult to navigate. There tends to be a societal 'unicorns and rainbows' misconception regarding this, the public attitude being, 'Oh well, you've found your birth parents – now you can skip hand in hand into the sunset and live happily ever after.' But it's not that simple.

Although thrilled to have my birth parents in my life, and to have met Elinor, I often felt overwhelmed and confused, teetering on a precipice between two mothers; Yvonne was my real mum, but I already had a 'mum' who'd raised me. I constantly felt stuck in the middle, trying to manage Mum's bitterness towards Yvonne while also considering my birth mother's feelings, recognising how she was desperately trying to make up for our years apart. Sometimes, I had to pull back slightly from my relationships with my birth parents, to protect my mental health.

I next saw Yvonne on 26 June 2004 – when she married Martin at St Benedict's Church in Northampton. She looked stunning in her dress, a voluminous princess-style gown with puffed sleeves, paired with a dainty tiara and flowing white veil.

I was four months pregnant then, not yet showing but highly emotional. I cried during Yvonne and Martin's vows and when I hugged her afterwards, I inhaled that same homely 'mother' smell that had lingered with me since we'd first met, which set me off again. 'Finding you has meant everything to me,' she told me, before I posed with her and Martin for a photograph outside the church. 'And now you're having a baby of your own – I can't tell you how proud I am to call myself a grandmother. You're going to be a great mum, Liz. I know you'll treasure every moment with your baby.'

I kissed her soft cheek. 'Ah, thanks Yvonne, and congratulations to you and Martin, too.' I wiped my eyes, then stood next to my birth mother and smiled at the camera.

* * *

Throughout my pregnancy I marvelled at the changes in my body – my growing bump, imagining our baby, developing little fingers and toes and tiny features inside me – and noted every occurrence in my pregnancy diary, including my cravings for citrus fruits and Rowntree's Fruit Pastilles.

Dan loved talking and singing to the baby. He'd rest his head on my bump and say things such as, 'Hello, Baby, it's your daddy here. We can't wait to meet you. You just be safe in there – you and Mummy look after each other. You're going to be so loved.'

As planned, we told the sonographer not to reveal the sex of our baby. We'd be overjoyed with a healthy boy or girl. Secretly – although I think Dan knew this at the time – I still yearned for a girl, a little version of me. Only recently did I realise the reason behind that strong urge: I wanted to go back and rescue myself as a vulnerable baby – to save 'Claire'.

Every step of my pregnancy fascinated me. Looking at my pregnancy diary today brings those months and precious memories flooding back:

8th June 2004
Week thirteen. Am obviously starting to 'show' today – some of the school mums kept looking at my tummy!

20th June 2004
Week fifteen: Father's Day. I made a card for the baby to give to Daddy and stuffed it up my nightie in bed in the morning. He loved it!

28th June 2004
Week sixteen. Had my check at the surgery with the midwife. Was able to listen to the baby's heartbeat. That made this all very real – I'm growing a person!

17 July 2004
Week eighteen. Baby was kicking like mad while we lay in bed tonight. Dan could actually FEEL the kicking against his

hand and his cheek! It's like they were communicating with one another!

28 November 2004
Felt very tired today. Only two weeks to go!

I remember writing that final entry at the end of November. By this stage, our baby was wriggling and punching and kicking day and night. It was mesmerising – albeit alien-like – to watch. I could see the shape of the baby's hands and feet pushing beneath my skin, the shape of its head, rolling this way and that.

As my due date rapidly approached, I tried to imagine what the birth would be like. I was the first woman in our friendship circle to fall pregnant – and I obviously couldn't ask Mum how labouring felt, what to expect. I was venturing into the unknown – but I was fully prepared with my birthing plan. During labour I'd listen to calming music and ocean and nature sounds while inhaling lavender oil. I'd even bought a TENS machine – a device that delivers pain relief via electrical impulses (I'd been told this would help when my contractions kicked in). In my head, my birth was going to be a magical, idyllic event – I couldn't wait to see my baby come out of my body. As an adoptee, this was so important to me.

And then …

Dan was at a work conference in Edinburgh when I went for my thirty-eight-week check-up on 30 November. It wasn't ideal for him to be far away from home so close to my due date, which was 12 December, but I still had two weeks to go, so we weren't too concerned. When the time finally came, though, there was no way on earth he wouldn't be there to help and support me in welcoming our baby into the world.

I arrived at the doctor's surgery around 5 p.m., heavily swollen, the baby doing a jig in my belly, heightening my excitement ahead of the birth.

My GP measured my bump and listened to the baby's heartbeat. Then she checked my blood pressure, which had been high for the past few weeks, but particularly so today – never a good sign at this late stage of pregnancy. My urine sample confirmed the doctor's concern. She looked at me over her glasses, an expression of urgency crossing her face. 'You have pre-eclampsia. There are two plus points of protein in your urine. This could seriously harm both you and your baby. Liz, this baby needs to come now.'

'Now? Today?' I heaved myself out of the chair.

'You'll need to go to the hospital right away. They'll need to induce you.'

I placed my hands protectively over my bump and the baby responded with a kick. *Thank you.*

'But my husband's not here. He's in Edinburgh. He *has* to be at the birth.' Terror coursed through my body. 'But I can't go straight to the hospital – I don't have my bag.'

'I suggest you get your bag quickly – the only solution is to get your baby out.'

I don't remember driving home, but when I got there, my bag was packed, there in the hallway, ready to go. Thank God my organisation had paid off. I called my friend Tracey, puffing as I explained my urgent situation.

'Okay, stay calm, Liz, I'm on my way – I'll drive you to the hospital.'

'Thanks Tracey,' I said, then went upstairs. *I don't know how long I'll be in hospital for. I need extra clothes.*

I phoned Dan as I frantically pulled items out of the drawers. 'Dan, you need to get home right now, there's an

emergency and the baby needs to come as soon as possible!'
I explained what the GP had told me, and that Tracey was on
her way.

'Okay, I'll be there as soon as I can,' he reassured me, 'Try
not to worry, darling.'

The doorbell chimed. 'Tracey's here, I've got to go. Please
drive carefully. I love you.'

* * *

Twenty minutes later, I was being induced in St Peter's Hospital,
Chertsey, the same hospital where Dan had undergone his
cancer treatment. Afterwards, I was left alone in a room to wait
for the medication to bring on my labour.

I plugged in my portable stereo and put on my ocean-sounds
CD, thinking, *This isn't what I was expecting.*

A few hours passed but nothing was happening. I still
hadn't gone into labour. I lay on the bed, listening to the
waves gently rolling in and out, inhaling my lavender oil.
*Where are the midwives? When will Dan be here? Will I have
to give birth alone?* My thoughts turned to Yvonne, alone in
the Barratt Maternity Home almost thirty years ago, waiting
to give birth to me, knowing that when I arrived, she'd be
forced to give me away. I imagined her loneliness, her fear,
her heartache.

At 2 a.m., griping pains surged through my belly. 'Why don't
you have a bath, take a couple of paracetamols,' advised one of
the ward nurses.

I waddled along the corridor to the bathroom, praying that Dan
would arrive soon. *This isn't what I was expecting.* I ran a bath
and slowly eased into it, but the hot water aggravated the pains

shooting through my lower stomach, and I felt a sudden urge to go to the toilet. I struggled out of the bath, wrapped a towel around me and hurried to the loo as fast as I could manage with my baby weight.

I recoiled in horror when I saw the contents in the toilet bowl: a thick black substance, like tar.

I yanked the emergency cord once, twice, three times. 'Help,' I yelled, 'we need help!' The treacly black liquid in the toilet bowl was meconium, my baby's first bowel movement – I'd read about this in my pregnancy books and knew that it meant that the baby was distressed. This was dangerous and potentially life-threatening for the baby if it were to aspirate or swallow the meconium.

What happened next happened fast. Nurses swarmed. I was bundled into a wheelchair and into a room where I was put onto a trolley and hastily examined. 'Mrs Harvie, you are very dilated now, but your baby is breech and it is presenting bottom-first. We need to get you down for an emergency C-section,' said one of the medics. My contractions were coming thick and fast as they rushed me out of the room and whizzed me so fast along the corridor that we bumped into the wall. I was given an epidural and taken into theatre. I was absolutely terrified. I remember asking the surgeon, 'Will I feel anything?'

'You might feel some tugging, but it won't be painful,' he said.

Dan arrived then, and it would've been a comical moment were it not for our emergency ordeal. 'They couldn't find any scrubs to fit me – again,' he said, sporting a green gown and overshoes at least ten sizes too small for him.

'Oh darling, thank goodness you're here.' I felt spaced out now and numb from the ribs downwards. I didn't know what to expect – I'd read all the books, but I'd been preparing for a natural, holistic birth, the one I'd dreamed of since I was a child. I was so frightened.

The curtain went up, concealing all the evidence I would have had that this baby was mine. Dan stood by my side, holding my hand while watching the surgery over the curtain. 'He's making the incision now. Do you want me to lift the curtain so you can see?'

I managed a weak smile. 'No, I don't think so, darling.'

The sensation was weird: lots of tugging as the surgeon had described – it felt like he was doing the washing up inside my abdomen.

'Nearly there,' said Dan, squeezing my hand.

I felt another tug, then heard suction noises. I looked up at Dan, but his eyes were trained on what was happening behind the screen, and they began to well with tears. 'Dan? Is everything okay?'

'Would you like to cut the cord?' the surgeon asked Dan.

Next, a cry. My baby's first cry. Dan nodded at the surgeon, then looked down at me, smiling and crying at once. 'You've got your baby Grace.'

I burst into tears. 'My baby Grace. I've got my baby Grace.'

Dan cut the umbilical cord. I'll never forget the next moment, when he lifted our beautiful daughter over the curtain. 'Hello, Grace Elizabeth Harvie,' I whispered. Dan lowered Grace onto my chest, and I kissed her soft damp hair. I couldn't stop staring at her; at her little button nose, her ten tiny fingers and toes. 'Oh Grace, you couldn't be more perfect.'

* * *

Grace was our world, our miracle. I cherished every moment with her, especially her first weeks and early months. The bond between us was unbreakable, everlasting. I could have looked at her forever. She had beautiful black shiny eyes, like little beads. I loved seeing her eyes lock with mine, feeling her skin against mine, and I held her with her heart pressed against mine, always.

I must admit, it distressed me when she cried. Every new mother instinctively knows their baby's cry – it's a primal recognition. Grace's cry sounded like a bleating newborn lamb. Some nights I'd wake up in a cold sweat when I heard her; my instinct to go to her, to feed her or cuddle her was so powerful. Rocking Grace in my arms, I'd think, *I must've needed my mother like you're needing me now.*

One of my fondest memories of Grace's baby days is of dancing around the lounge with her to the song 'Ms Grace' by the seventies band The Tymes. I'd put that track on every afternoon and bop her up and down in my arms, singing along. She'd giggle and smile and wriggle her little legs. That was our thing. Our special moment, mother and daughter.

When Grace was seven months old, Dan dropped an unexpected bombshell.

'Erm, we need to have a little chat,' he announced over dinner one evening.

I put down my knife and fork; this sounded serious. 'Really? What about? Is everything okay?'

'How do you feel about moving to Belgium?'

'Belgium?'

'My boss approached me today, asking whether I'd consider taking up a new position there in the European Headquarters in Brussels.'

'That's great news, well done, darling.' I was proud that his company valued him so much, but the prospect of upheaval from somewhere so familiar was daunting; we'd need to consider it practically. 'But Grace is only seven months old and we're settled here. I've made close friends with my antenatal buddies, so has Grace, with the other babies.' I felt comfortable and welcomed at the mother-and-baby groups in Egham. I felt secure in our home, in Englefield Green, where we'd made so many memories since our university days.

'I understand how you're feeling, darling. I know this is a big decision. I'll miss it here too! But I'm sure there'll be lots of similar groups in Belgium – and you're always saying you wish you could use your French more. It's a great opportunity for us as a family, and it'll only be for two years.'

Moving to Belgium began to feel like a more feasible option for us. After all, Grace was only young, and perhaps she too could develop some French. I had really missed using mine. 'But what will we do with the house?'

Dan sipped his wine, thinking for a moment. 'Well, we don't have to decide straight away. We can just mull it over for now.'

After much deliberating, we decided to take a leap of faith and go for the job in Belgium. As Dan had pointed out, living abroad would be an exciting opportunity for us as a young family, and only for a short period of time.

In January 2006, just after Grace's first birthday, we packed up our home, which we'd decided to rent out while in Belgium, and moved to Wezembeek-Oppem, a picturesque municipality on the outskirts of Brussels.

We rented a house in a quiet, traditional neighbourhood where on Sunday the shops closed and nobody mowed their gardens. The pace of life was slower than at home, which I liked, but it was tough sometimes. Dan had to travel for work around seventy per cent of the time, so he was away from home a lot, which was incredibly difficult for me, looking after baby Grace mostly on my own.

I enjoyed speaking French again, and I quickly made friends with other mums, growing to love our new surroundings. I'd spend my days at mother-and-baby groups with Grace or perusing the many food markets in town. The seasons slipped by.

During our first autumn in Belgium, I fell pregnant again. It took me by surprise how quickly I'd conceived this time around – we laughed when we realised it must have happened while we were holidaying in France. 'Conceived in France, born in Belgium,' Dan joked. We were thrilled – Grace would soon have a little brother or sister.

I clung to the hope of a second chance at giving birth naturally. My opportunity to see Grace coming out of my body had been taken away from me in such a dramatic fashion; I was still struggling with that. Shortly after Grace's birth, I spoke to a therapist at the post-birth counselling service at the hospital, but my words had fallen on deaf ears. She didn't understand how traumatic it can be for an adoptee to give birth, not to mention my stolen chance to see my baby being born.

Fortunately, I didn't have to endure the same emergency procedure with my second baby. Despite one medical incident, I gave birth to her naturally. It was the most magical experience – also, almost entirely in French. On 24 June 2007, we welcomed Isabel Charlotte Harvie, our beautiful second daughter, into the world. She was perfect, just like her sister.

We ended up staying in Belgium for six-and-a-half years as Dan continued to soar through the ranks at work, promotion following promotion. But, in 2012, we were ready to come home, our lives enriched by new experiences, happy memories and two precious children.

It felt strange at first being back; I had to remind myself not to speak in French. Grace spoke fluent French too after attending a local school in Belgium. She had a lovely authentic accent. For a while, we welcomed French back into our English at home, speaking in our own blend of the two languages.

Not one day passed without my feeling so blessed for my family, our girls; being a mum was all that I'd ever wanted, but my adoption trauma still haunted me. Often, I'd visualise the nursery at the Barratt Maternity Home. I'd see Claire, crying in her bassinet, or Yvonne, a tear running down her cheek as she stared through the nursery window, forbidden from comforting her baby.

Over the following two years, I attended various counselling sessions as I tried to navigate my path through The Fog – a process my adoptive parents simply couldn't comprehend. My relationship with Mum was becoming increasingly strained – unbearable at times. But her behaviour on my fortieth birthday was abominable, spiteful and would lead ultimately to the breakdown of our relationship for good.

I had arranged a party for my fortieth: a milestone that should be celebrated in style, I thought. I've always loved vintage clothes and jewellery – a passion that stems back to my childhood memories of playing with Nanny Mac's trinkets – so I decided on a 1940s' theme for my celebration. '1940s' attire, or we will not let you in,' I wrote, only half-jokingly, on the invitations.

Yvonne, Martin and Andy would be attending, along with Mum and Dad and a cast of forty-odd friends. My adoptive parents would finally meet Yvonne and Andy. And, although this interaction would certainly bring a range of emotions and reactions, this was my party, my choice – and I wanted my birth parents there ón my special day.

Mum and Dad arrived the day before my party, as did Yvonne, Martin and Andy, who were staying at a nearby hotel.

We'd arranged to go for lunch with all five of them, and a group of my closest friends, to get my celebrations underway.

At The Half Moon pub in Windlesham, I introduced my adoptive parents to Yvonne and Andy. It seemed to go relatively smoothly, but, over lunch, I caught Mum narrowing her eyes at my birth mother.

After we'd eaten, Yvonne handed me a birthday card. 'Now, I know it's not your birthday until tomorrow,' she said, 'but you can open it now if you'd like.'

'That's so sweet. Thanks, Yvonne.' I decided to open the card at the table, sensing Mum's gaze burning holes through the envelope.

As always, the message on the front of the card read, *For My Wonderful Daughter*.

Yvonne smiled, dipping her head, as she does. 'Oh, and here's a little pressie for you, too.' She handed me a small box.

'Oh, Yvonne, you shouldn't have,' I said. I was touched by this gesture; she was trying to make my day as special as she could after all the birthdays she had missed out on.

As I unwrapped my present, Mum shifted awkwardly in her seat. She was sitting directly opposite me, next to Dad. 'Have you seen what's on that card?' she said to Dad, a comment just loud enough for those closest to us to notice.

Dad tried to diffuse the situation. 'Well, she is her mother – that's how she sees Elizabeth.'

My face burned. *How dare she – in front of Yvonne.* I opened the box – she had bought me a beautiful charm for my bracelet, the one I wore almost every day. But, before I could thank her, Mum chimed in again.

'Come and show me what you got, Elizabeth,' she demanded. Once more, she couldn't bring herself to say Yvonne's name. I thanked Yvonne for her lovely gift, and the conversation swiftly changed around the table, but I was furious at Mum.

The following evening, my birthday party was underway at The Brickmakers, a gastro pub in Windlesham, Surrey. I'd had so much fun planning the event and styling the venue. I decorated the rich claret walls with wartime posters, strung Union Jack garlands, and scattered the tables with ration books and vintage rail tickets.

Everyone had gone to a huge effort to look the part. I wore a 1940s' classic black dress and fur stole, which I had rented from a theatre hire shop. I styled my hair in victory rolls, wore ruby red lipstick and round my neck I proudly wore one of my dear Nanny Mac's necklaces.

Andy looked amazing, dressed as a colonel – he'd even grown a hefty silver moustache for the occasion. Yvonne wore a black-and-white polka-dot dress with chiffon sleeves and an elegant vintage pearl necklace. I'd seated my birth parents and Martin at a table with my neighbours: warm, friendly people who I knew would put them at ease. I wanted the three of them to feel comfortable.

It was such a fun evening, everyone posing for photographs in their costumes, the hum of conversations and laughter mingling with wartime music.

After dinner, I stood up to make a speech, which had taken much time and effort to compose. This was a proud, important moment for me, and everybody turned to listen. I began by thanking my guests for coming to my party and making it such a special occasion, especially those who had travelled a long way to be there, with me. I gave a nod to the costumes; everyone had put so much effort into looking the part. I held my breath for a moment before continuing with the more personal part of my message.

'Some of you in this room may not know this, but I'm adopted. I never thought this moment would come, that I would be sharing my past at my fortieth birthday party.' Many of my

214

friends didn't know about my adoption; I hadn't told them. My beginnings had been, as always, unspoken. Now, I wanted my voice to be heard. The room fell silent.

I faltered, but continued, allowing the tears to fall freely down my face. 'I'm so privileged to be able to tell you all that my birth mother and father are actually here in this room this evening. For the first time, I have all four of my parents in the same room at the same time – a very special moment.' A series of gasps rippled through the air, people turning to look around the room. Yvonne clasped her hands over to her heart and looked at me, her bottom lip quivering. Andy gave me a gentle smile.

'I'm hugely thankful to my adoptive parents for all the opportunities they have afforded me, but this evening, I'd like to introduce you to my *birth* parents, Yvonne and Andy.' I beckoned for them to join me. Yvonne and Andy stood up, though hesitantly, and came to me. The room erupted with supportive applause. Then the three of us came together in the tightest hug you could imagine. There I was, in the arms of my birth parents, a moment I thought I would never experience. Pain forgotten, our missing years cast aside, just for a few moments of gentle warmth and connection between us.

I breathed the scent of my birth mother, as she croaked, 'I love you.' Then nobody spoke. We just stood there, enveloped in each other.

No words were needed. The truth of my beginnings, my history, was out there.

Finally spoken.

Epilogue

Lifelong Trauma

Camberley, Surrey, Thursday 15 June 2023
I was in the kitchen making American pancakes for my daughter Izzy when I found out that my adoptive mother had died.

Dan broke the news to me in a phone call from his business trip in Seoul, South Korea.

I'd smiled when his name flashed on the screen along with the heart emoji I'd assigned to his contact – I'm always happy to receive an unscheduled call from Dan, especially when he's away.

'Hi, my love, how are you? Lovely to hear from you. I'm making pancakes for Izzy and me,' I gushed, whisking the batter.

'Not too bad, thanks – the pancakes sound good, but, darling, can you sit down?'

'What do you mean?'

'I just need you to sit down for a minute please.'

I perched on the bar stool, still holding the whisk. 'Dan, you're worrying me now. Is everything okay? Are you alright?'

He paused. 'Your mum's died.'

A jolt shuddered through me like an electric shock. I shot from the stool, sending the whisk crashing to the floor, batter splattering the cupboard. My heart pounded, my breath hurried, then I let out a wail resembling the cry of a wounded animal. I wanted to speak but I couldn't form words – only this haunting, primal sound escaped my mouth.

Dan stayed silent until my cries subsided, giving me space to try to take all this in. Then questions tumbled from my mouth.

'What the hell … she's *dead?* What happened? How come *you're* telling me this, not Dad or my brother? Who's told you? And *when?*'

Dan said my brother's wife had broken the news of my mother's death to him. Mum had passed away in the early hours of this morning after suffering a stroke a few days beforehand. 'Your brother and his wife were with him. So was your dad.' *They hadn't told me.* Despite my agreement with my brother, that he would tell me should a serious end-of-life emergency happen, he had allowed our father to dictate everything – that I wasn't to be informed until after she had died, that I wasn't to be told when the funeral was and that I would not be welcome at it. I was utterly shocked.

Izzy came into the kitchen then and intuitively gave me a hug. She was whispering questions, and although I couldn't respond, I sensed she'd heard enough to know what had happened.

'Back in a minute,' she said, and hurried away. I later found out she'd heard everything and had gone to call Grace.

I calmed down a bit, came back into my body. I sat on the sofa and Wilson, my eldest dog, jumped up and rested his head in my lap. That dog always knows when something is up. I stroked him slowly and rhythmically, noticing my emotions, or lack of them, rising to the surface.

'You know, darling – this sounds awful, but I just feel numb. I don't mean that I'm numbing my feelings. I just feel … nothing, just … a flatline, you know?'

'Yep. I know.'

'No, actually I feel peace. Does that sound bad? I think it's relief. She's gone. It's finished. No more.' My voice was now calm, measured, the tightness in my chest had dissipated. That's exactly how I felt. It was over. She could no longer hurt me.

'I feel that too, and it's *okay* for you to feel that – it really is.'

* * *

A quiet calm passed through me and I decided that the right thing to do was to reach out to both my brother and father with condolences. In the days and weeks to come, their responses would cause the total breakdown of their relationships with me. The letter that came through the post from my father took the breath right out of my chest, his words saturated with anger, accusations and spite. Both my brother and father had stated in writing that they did not wish to see me again.

Dan had supported me through all of this, including my grappling with numbness at the death itself. He too had endured my mother, witnessed her being unreasonable, uncaring, jealous and at times downright cruel to me. None of these words resonated with 'mother' to me.

Dan had frequently dealt with the aftermath of her bitterness, her demands, her ruining of special occasions or visits and her need for public perfection. He'd endured countless car journeys back from Mum and Dad's, seeing me in floods of tears after being around her toxicity. It didn't belong in our world. It was poisonous – to an unbearable degree.

In September 2022, I was forced to establish a boundary and estrange myself from my mother. I justified my reasons to them; I explained that it had affected my mental health, that I needed to protect myself, so that I could take the time and space I really needed to heal. Not only from my lifelong trauma of forced adoption, but from the detrimental consequences of my mother's behaviour towards me. Grace and Izzy had been exposed to this too, and were old enough to make their own minds up about her as a person. No child should need protecting and keeping away from their grandmother, but that's what we had to do – for me, for them, for all four of us.

Over the next few days and weeks after my mother's death, anger and resentment began to surface. I was confused by those conflicting emotions. My lack of sadness was another challenge I had to confront head on, so I tried to be gentle with myself as I learnt to cope with my loss. And the more time I spent grieving, the more I became aware of its multifaceted nature; I realised I was also grieving the loss of the mother I *needed*. I had to tell myself that feeling a variety of emotions, including numbness, at her death was understandable in my situation. I am still trying to come to a place of acceptance.

In April 2023, I was diagnosed with CPTSD (Complex Post Traumatic Stress Disorder). At the time of writing I am undergoing EMDR (Eye Movement Desensitization and Reprocessing), which is considered the gold standard treatment for helping people to recover from trauma. It's brutal.

This psychotherapy treatment uses eye movements, audio tones and/or vibrating hand-held buzzers to stimulate the left and right sides of the brain to aid processing and integration of traumatic memories, to access them as simply memories, without suffering a distressing reaction or negative feelings when we recall or discuss whatever has traumatised us.

Most of us have heard of PTSD, and we often associate it with war veterans, but it can also arise from a single traumatic incident (an assault, traumatic childbirth, a fire, an accident etc.). CPTSD occurs as a result of long-term trauma, particularly when the initial trauma has been pre-verbal, experienced during the early stages of development.

This is because at such an early age, a child's neurological and cognitive abilities have not yet fully developed.

Until I did my own research and educated myself on preverbal trauma, developmental trauma, childhood trauma and its effects on my body, I didn't understand what was happening. I just thought there was something wrong with me.

When I finally understood what my body had been doing for all these years, I felt a new-found tenderness and empathy for it. It had simply been trying to protect me all along. The sheer panic and terror I must have felt at being separated from my mother at barely ten days old, of her being replaced with a foster mother for eight weeks, and then a permanent 'other mother' – it's no wonder all these trauma reactions had been raging inside me.

My therapist took me right back to my first ten days of life, in the hospital, with my mother. My brain cannot recall the memory of those days, but I know my body remembers it.

With my eyes shut and the EMDR buzzers held tightly in each hand, buzzing back and forth to activate both hemispheres of my brain, she led me back there, to that hospital, bringing steadily to life the information my birth mother Yvonne has since told me about my early days.

I saw the four-bed hospital ward Yvonne had stayed in. I saw balloons, cards, flowers, so many flowers. I heard ripples of laughter, the high-pitched tones of joyous conversations of families visiting, cooing over their newborns. But not for Yvonne: she was alone, head down, her bedside devoid of visitors or anything celebratory. There was nothing around her to signify something happy and deeply wanted had happened. *Where was newborn me?*

My therapist gently guided me, the buzzers still oscillating back and forth, left and right, as I ventured tentatively to the nursery, where they held the babies who were 'not for keeping'. They had been flagged for adoption, and it was standard practice to keep those shamed mothers and their unknowing newborns apart for periods (to reduce bonding). This was a devastating time for the mothers, and very damaging to us babies. 'First do no harm' – *Whatever happened to that?*

I recognised the nursery because Yvonne had described it to me in the past, but I had put it at the back of my mind until this particular session.

I started sobbing. Heavy, wet tears fell onto the buzzers I held tightly in my lap. My shoulders shook.

'What's coming up now, Liz?' my therapist asked softly.

I paused and tried to listen to what my body was pushing to the surface, from forty-nine years of secrets buried deep within me. 'I'm just so very sad, and angry.'

Then I couldn't speak. I looked down at baby Claire, feeling our thoughts, emotions and selves morph into one, trying to intuit and give voice to what she could never express. Only disjointed words came, as if they had been spoken to me by Claire herself. *Lost. Alone. Unloved. Unlovable. Terrified. Nobody's coming. Who are you? I need my mother. Where is she?*

'It's OK, Liz. Just breathe.'

I have to get to Claire. I open the nursery door and hurry past the maternity nurses. I reach down and pick Claire up, bringing her to my chest, pulling her in close to my body. She stops crying, and so do I. She nuzzles into my neck, and I take in a jagged breath.

Here we are, me and my newborn self, meeting in another dimension, this safe space, guided by my trauma therapist sitting opposite me, helping me access these locked-in memories.

I hold Claire.

'What are you feeling now, Liz?'

'I'm doing better now.' The initial feeling of distress at looking at or even thinking of myself in that bassinet having originally been a 9/10. 'She's okay when I'm there with her. I want to take her with me.'

'So take her with you. Tell her you'll look after her, that it's not her fault.'

It's not her fault.

Fresh tears rolled down my cheeks, making tracks through the dried ones I'd shed earlier; this was not pretty work. I put my head to one side, somehow trying to look away from it all. My latest tears tasted different, of something like iodine. They must have come from somewhere very deep.

It seemed to take a good while, sitting very still, my therapist having slowed down the pace of the buzzers, to settle back into my body, Claire still with me somewhere.

* * *

I'm one of 185,000 victims, a conservative estimate, of forced adoption between 1949 and 1976 in England and Wales. Yvonne was deemed unfit as a parent by her father, and, like so many other unsupported women, by the government, by the church, by both state and church Moral Welfare Officers, by adoption agencies, and therefore made to give me up against her will.

On 23 September 2021, an inquiry by the Joint Committee on Human Rights into The Right To Family Life – Adoption of Children of Unmarried Women 1974–1976 was announced. Many adoptees bravely gave oral, written and round-table evidence to the inquiry, on their lived experience of forced adoption.

I found myself in parliament, giving evidence as a victim of forced adoption. This inquiry gave adult adoptees the chance to be heard, to share our stories and, in doing so, have our struggles acknowledged and validated. For most of us, it was the very first time that we had ever spoken out about our adoption experiences.

It was both empowering and terrifying, yet in the knowledge that many of our adoptee community were doing the same in opening up and sharing our stories, a collective confidence started to grow.

In May 2022, after meeting each other for the first time after this inquiry, I came together with six other female adoptees to found the Adult Adoptee Movement. I feel honoured and proud to be a part of this group; I feel like, finally, I have found my 'tribe'.

We have a wealth of diverse, rich, lived experience, which remains at the heart of everything we do. We aim to raise adoptee voices, advocate for adoptee rights, raise awareness of the lifelong impact of adoption that adoptees face, and to ensure that appropriate support is available to all those affected, both in terms of mental health, tracing our relatives and accessing our birth and medical records.

The Adult Adoptee Movement challenges societal attitudes towards historic adoptions, highlights unacceptable practices and strives to change the narrative on adoption. With many other adoptees who have helped our group along the way, we are making big strides. Most importantly to us, we also aim to create safe spaces, where all adoptees can feel seen, heard and validated.

In October 2021, we collated a hefty document in response to the JCHR inquiry report, setting out fourteen recommendations, which we distributed far and wide to MPs, journalists, counselling bodies, other adoptee activist groups, charities, lawyers and influencers.

As I write this, in August 2023, we are still waiting for the UK government to follow Scotland and Wales in issuing a formal apology for its undeniably pertinent role in forced adoption. Despite the existence of plenty of archival evidence proving otherwise, the current government continues to maintain that it was 'society' which was to blame, that the government itself had no involvement in this shameful historic practice. Although it would be amazing to get an apology, in terms of validation and recognising that what was done to us was abhorrent and, importantly, at the hands of the State, it would still only be the beginning. For us, it is more about action – not just for present-day adult adoptees, but for the many adoptees who come behind us.

Our journey continues.

Acknowledgements

Writing this book about my lifelong trauma as a forced adoptee has certainly been a cathartic process. I have experienced so many different emotions and processed so many memories that I would go as far as to say it has been a kind of spiritual experience for me.

There are times when it has proved extremely challenging. I have experienced deep sadness – over lost years, lost connections and lost identities. There have been significant moments of grief, a disenfranchised grief which society cannot fathom, one not socially or publicly supported. One which adoptees are forbidden to feel – the loss of biological connection, genetic mirroring. There have been moments of anger, rage and defiance at times, partly towards the UK government which separated so many babies from their mothers. As I write this in August 2023, the current government continues to maintain that it was 'society' which was to blame, that the government itself had no involvement in forced adoption, refusing to issue a formal apology for its undeniably pertinent role in this shameful historic practice.

There have been times when I have had to search my subconscious, digging deep for memories, experiences and feelings that I had buried. And when I retrieved them, I had no choice but to relive them all over again. This process was, at times, ugly. It compares to intense trauma therapy, all without the guidance of a therapist alongside me.

But there have also been some beautiful, positive moments in the writing of this book, as I recalled happy, poignant memories. It has been a form of therapy for me, a vehicle through which I can express and process my trauma – it goes hand in hand with my EMDR treatment. And now that I feel my voice has been afforded the space to be heard, there has also been acknowledgement, validation and a slow and steady movement towards acceptance – not only of what has happened to me, but of myself.

My heartfelt thanks go to my co-author Nicola Stow who has worked so intimately and intensely with me on this book. We've spent months together on Zooms or phone calls – interviews given, memories imparted, stories told, documents, records and old photographs shared, in order for Nicola to 'become' me for the duration of this book. Nic, you've not only been my co-author, but you have also listened and been witness to my life story as a forced adoptee. You have sensitively and empathically held space when the content became a little too much, but we have also shared much laughter too and for all of the above, I am truly thankful to you.

I give special thanks and acknowledgment to my birth mother Yvonne, who has also invested her time and emotional energy in the writing of this book. I appreciate that it has been hard for you to relive your experiences in these pages. I am beyond fortunate to have reunited with you.

To my birth father Andy, also very much a part of my story. Thank you for your authenticity, and for allowing me to share our experience together. I cherish the connection we share.

Deserving of a special mention is Jo Sollis, former Mardle Books publisher – without you noticing me in the media, my musings on Twitter and my involvement in adoptee advocacy, this book would never have happened in the first place. Thank you for having the confidence in me to allow me to share my story.

My thanks go to Mardle Books, to everyone who has been involved in bringing my story to life, but huge thanks go especially to the following: Duncan Proudfoot, editorial director, deadline-checker and general project manager; Rob Nichols, who worked on the cover and copy. To my publicist Mel Sambells, Kaz Harrison in marketing, Gill Woolcott in production, and to Jon Rippon. To the sales team also. Thank you to you all.

To my friends, who have been so supportive, not only of me writing this book, but throughout the journey that has gone alongside it. Thank you. Very special thanks go to you, Hannah.

To my cofounders of the Adult Adoptee Movement. I can't even begin to put into words how much I value and cherish each and every one of you ladies. United by our shared experience as forced adoptees, we have shared so much – sadness, heartache, frustration and anger, but also laughter and joy. The empathy and support we have for each other is such that often no words are needed among us – we can read and interpret each other like a book – knowing when one of us is down, struggling, needing to take a step back from advocacy and campaigning while the others step up/hold the fort, making ourselves available for a Zoom in a personal crisis, or just being there to listen. It is hugely validating for me to have you in my life. I will be eternally grateful for your friendship and our sense of community. Heartfelt thanks to all of you.

To my fellow adoptees, first and foremost, I want to acknowledge the diversity of the adoptee experience. There is a very broad range of life experiences within our community: transracial adoptees; transnational adoptees; intercountry adoptees; adoptees who have lost their heritage, their culture; adoptees who have no access to their information, their medical history; adoptees whose records are redacted or access restricted by the state, records apparently destroyed in a fire, a flood ... or a plague of locusts; late-discovery adoptees; adoptees who 'find' their mothers only to discover that they have died; adoptees who find their first families on the other side of the planet, speaking a different language; adoptees whose reunions are problematic, which may even 'fail'; adoptees who experience secondary rejection by their birth mothers; adoptees who were abused, in any way; adoptees who are estranged by choice from their adoptive and/or birth families; adoptees who live with mental health conditions; adoptees who are addicts – we are, as a community, over-represented in the mental health system and in treatment facilities and prisons; adoptees who are in such pain that they either attempt to end their own life, or succeed in doing so. And so it goes on – a truly diverse collection of experiences and people. I neither intend nor claim to speak for them all; I am merely one voice in this community, sharing *my* story. I also recognise that not all adoptees will acknowledge or deal with this trauma in the same way. Some may simply not feel the effects, some may feel healed by their upbringing. Some may doubt or deny its existence, others may block it out, perhaps a form of self-preservation, and all of this is okay. After all, the brain does a great job of protecting us from this trauma by attempting to sweep it away from our conscious memory. But the science behind this trauma and its effects cannot be denied.

Despite our different experiences, we all share one thing in common: we were all separated from our mothers, from our kin – severed legally and permanently. We all experienced the internal shock of that separation, whether we are willing and able to acknowledge it or not. We were entered into a lifelong contract without our consent. Our right to family life and our human rights were violated. We all live with society's adoption narrative which tells us to be grateful, that we were chosen, special, that we were given a 'better' life. And while this may well be the case for some, personally, I struggled with society's expectations of my experience as an adoptee all my life.

I would like adoptees to know that you are all valid, that you have a voice that should be heard, that every one of you is meant to be here, that you are loved beyond measure by your 'people' – even if you haven't found them yet – they are out there. (Those who will support you best may be friends, other adoptees, mentors, therapists …) I sincerely hope you find them, and I hope that my book encourages you to find your voice.

I hope that my book reaches those adoptees who are feeling alone, who think they are the only one, who are wondering if they should try to find their families, who are struggling with reunion. I hope these pages let you know that you are not alone, that there are hundreds of thousands of us out here. We are all survivors of adoption. And together, I hope we can start to heal.

As Bell Hooks said, 'Rarely, if ever, are any of us healed in isolation. Healing is an act of communion.'

The Adult Adoptee Movement
We are a group of UK adoptees, challenging attitudes to historic adoptions, striving to change the narrative on adoption. We campaign to ensure adult adoptee voices are heard, and better support processes are in place. If you'd like to sign up to

our newsletter to stay informed of the latest developments, you can do so via our website below.

Website: adultadoptee.org.uk
Email: adultadopteemovement@gmail.com
Twitter: @AdultAdopteeMov
Facebook: www.facebook.com/AdultAdopteeMov